ARE YOU A

BORN AGAIN CHRISTIAN

OR A

SO-CALLED ONE?

ODANY AUGUSTIN

International Standard Book Number: 1-59872-671-3

CONTENTS

Dedication

This book is dedicated to all born again Christians around the world who are not ashamed of the gospel of Jesus Christ, and who live the Christian life with faith, love and hope, also with obedience and faithfulness to the commandments of Jesus Christ in every aspect of their lives to accomplish the great commission and bring to pass the physical Kingdom of Jesus Christ for the glory of God.

It's also dedicated to the future Christians whom the Lord will call to know Him one way or another.

May your Christian life be what the Lord intended it to be, so that the name of our Master may be glorified!

May the call of Jesus Christ to the future Christians be sweet and tender, so that no one can turn it down!

And may His love, peace and joy be with you throughout your earthly life until the day you enter His presence in paradise!

"I am coming soon. Hold on to what you have, so that no one take your crown."

Revelation 3:11

Notice.

I.   The word Christian or Born Again Christian will be used when speaking about the authentic believer, and the word So-Called Christian will be used when referring to the non-believer affiliated in some way with a church.

II.   The scripture references are from the New International Version of the Bible **(NIV),** unless otherwise stated.

III.   If you did not take the Christian test, I would encourage you to do so before you read this book. Simply go to **www.thechristiantest.com.**

The Ten Commandments

"The Jewish and Christian official Moral code"

1. You shall have no other gods before Me.
2. You shall not make for yourself a carved image; nor shall you bow down or serve them.
3. You shall not take the name of the Lord your God in vain.
4. Remember the Sabbath day, to keep holy.
5. Honor your father and your mother that your days may be long upon the land.
6. You shall not murder.
7. You shall not commit adultery
8. You shall not steal
9. You shall not bear false witness against your neighbor.
10. You shall not covet your neighbor's things.

NKJV.

The Greatest Commandment according to Jesus.

1. Love the Lord your God with all your heart and with all your soul and with all your mind and with all your strength.

2. Love your neighbor as yourself.

   There is no Commandment greater than these." Mark 12:30, 31

-Acknowledgements-

I am grateful to God who has saved me, blessed me and called me to the ministry where I find the inspiration to write.

I want to express my appreciation:

- To the faithful and loyal leaders and members of "Bethesda Christian Center" (the church that I serve), who have shown their love to me with intelligent gifts such as books, and words engraved on plaques and printed in cards.

- To my former professor and adviser, Pastor James Montgomery and Family. Your dedication and sacrifices with your family are deeply appreciated.

- To my father and mother, Emmanuel & Phoenia Augustin, two authentic Christians who at a very early age taught me the fear of the Lord.

- My deepest appreciation goes to my wife, Marie Jose, who has supported this project whole heartedly and also put these materials in print, and to our three wonderful children, Dyona, Josie, Onesiphore (whom we are delighted to be the parents), who assisted anyway they can in the research of this document.

"May the Lord who began this good work in them carry it on to completion until the day of Jesus Christ!"
Philippians 1:6

RECIPE

Dear friend, would you like to have a good day?
Here is a Recipe that can help you!

To be prepared every morning:

2 cups of prayer
2 deciliters of patience
1 cup of kindness
4 teaspoons of good will
4 pinches of hope
1 dose of good faith

ALSO ADD

2 handfuls of tolerance
3 packets of prudence
A few sprigs of sympathy
2 handfuls of humility
1 big measure of good humor
Season with a good amount of common sense
Let it simmer and you'll get
A GOOD DAY

ANONYMOUS

Introduction

Are you a born again Christian or a so-called one?

In the beginning of Christianity it was not important to distinguish between born-again Christians and so-called ones, since there was no such group. The risks were too high for somebody to fake Christianity in the first century. Three times the followers of Christ were called Christians in the New Testament. (Acts 11:26; 26:28; I Peter 4:16). Twice the use of the term Christian came from unbelievers. First-century Christians were without a shadow of a doubt born again Christians. It was not necessary to add the word born again, because there were no so-called Christians at that time.

However, things have changed. If you say today: I am a Christian without adding some kind of adjective, like: authentic, born again, Evangelical and so on, you might be identified as a hypocrite, an adulterer, a dishonest person and the list goes on.

We might ask the question: Why?

I am going to give you some reasons:

1. Today people call themselves Christians because they are not Muslims, Buddhists, Indus, or some other major religion.

2. They consider themselves Christians because they live in a so-called Christian nation (which is, however, difficult to find today).

3. They call themselves Christians for convenience or to gain some personal advantage.

4. Some call themselves Christians because they were born in a Christian family. Being a Christian for them is only part of

their heritage. Do you know that many communist leaders and atheists were born in a Christian family?

These are some reasons why people call themselves Christians. Meanwhile, if you were to ask them a few questions, you would figure out quickly that they are nothing of the sort. They do not know the meaning of being a Christian. They are ignorant of who Jesus Christ is. Being a Christian for them is going to church once a month, or every Christmas and Easter. However, the true believer knows very well that being a Christian is something completely different than that.

Notice that I say "the true believer, not the true Christian." I do not believe in the adjective true in front of Christian, because there is no false Christian in my opinion; you are either a born again Christian or you are a hypocrite. The title Christian implies a vital personal relationship with Christ Himself. So if you are born again, then you are a follower of Christ or a Christian, if not, you are nothing.

The only person worthy to carry the title Christian is a true representative of Jesus Christ. In other words, if somebody in a far country has only heard or read about Jesus Christ's life but then meets a born-again Christian for the first time, he should be able (even when casually observing this Christian's actions and words) to recognize him or her as a real Christian! Why? Because of the way you act, the way you talk, the way you behave. They should be able to see the reflection of Jesus Christ in your life as a disciple of Jesus Christ.

My objectives in this book are to:

1. Establish the difference between a born again Christian and a so-called one.
2. Help everybody to truly identify themselves (as protestant, Catholic, pagan, etc… but not Christian, until they decide to become one).

3. Help people to stop misusing the title Christian.

4. Encourage those who are Christians to persevere and to demonstrate their real identity as Christians every day by their actions; and encourage the ones who want to become Christians to step forward and do it boldly and clearly by being born again, filled with the Holy Spirit of God and living the Christian life victoriously for Christ's sake. As Christians, we must apply the teachings of the Bible to our lives. We cannot believe in evolution or in any other human theory. We must hold onto creationism.

The history of God's people, the Israelites, should be of much interest to us. The Triune God of Abraham, Isaac and Jacob is the only True God, and by following the instructions he gave to His people we will live a life that is pleasing to Him and that will bring all kind of blessings upon us.

Men must acknowledge that we are all sinners, and that only by faith in the sacrifice of Jesus Christ, the Lamb of God, can we be saved.

"Salvation is found in no one else, for there is no other name under heaven given to men by whom we must be saved."

Every believer is obligated (by order of the Lord Himself) to be a member of a local church. No Christian can defy the commands of his master. It is to be or not to be. The true believer has only one master, the Lord Jesus Christ. If you serve money instead of God or try to serve both, then you are not born again as yet. It is mandatory to model our lives after Jesus Christ. The Ten Commandments are the highest moral code there is, and they come from the mouth of God. God is the highest moral character there is, and man is the lowest. Therefore, as Christians, we must follow God's model, not man's.

I do acknowledge that there are new, weak, and carnal Christians according to the Bible, but even in the lives of such people, others must be able to see some fruits of Christianity.

CHAPTER ONE

THE BIBLE

1. What is *the* Bible?

Psalm 1:1-2: *"Blessed is the man who does not walk in the counsel of the wicked or stand in the way of sinners or sit in the seat of mockers. But his delight is in the law of the Lord, and on his law he meditates day and night."* (NIV)

A young boy once noticed a big book covered with dust in the library in his house and he asked his mother: "What is this, Mommy?" "Oh, it is a Bible. It is the Book of God." The boy thinks for a minute and says:
"If it is the Book of God, why don't you give it back to Him? Nobody makes use of it here!" [1]

No matter what people think, say, or do with the Bible, it remains the most important book which has ever existed in the history of mankind. The Bible is from the Greek word Biblia, which means the books.

The Bible is called the Book of books, which is perfectly right since the Bible is not only a compilation of many books, but also the most extraordinary Book that has ever existed. The Bible is superior to all other written documents.

"The protestant Bible consists of sixty six books, of which thirty-nine belong to the Old Testament and twenty-seven to the New Testament. In the Roman Catholic versions, which follow the Vulgate, an additional fourteen apocryphal books are included." [2]

The Bible was written over a period of approximately 1,500 years by about 40 inspired men of God, which means they only held the "pen" and "paper", but God told them what to write.

Sometime ago, I was listening to a Christian radio station and I heard someone define the Bible as: "Basic instructions before leaving Earth." This is very creative and has a profound truth in it. I encourage you to think about that definition of the Bible and make sure to receive these instructions before your departure from this earth.

The Bible is the infallible, inerrant word of God. If you are looking for a piece of literature that cannot fail or one with no error, then the Bible is what you are looking for. Because the Bible is God breathed, it is infallible and inerrant, and no other book is like the Bible.

The Bible is also the book of knowledge. No man comes close to real knowledge apart from knowing God; and God has revealed Himself in the Bible. The Bible declares that: *"the fear of the Lord is the beginning of wisdom."* (Proverbs.9: 10) In other words, if you knew all about the whole world (about all the nations, civilizations, heads of states and their military secrets, their riches and culture and so on), you would still fall short of true knowledge, because you would not yet know God and His word.

You may have in your possession right now many degrees, including one or more Ph D's... but, do you know that if you do not know God and His word, you probably don't know what is going to happen to you five minutes after you die, though you might have some intimation but not a certain conviction. This is how little you know without the real knowledge which is found only in the Book of books.

In order for you to begin having knowledge, you must first know God, and the only way to know Him is to go to the Bible, by first acknowledging Jesus Christ as your personal Savior.

Here is one of the most profound definitions of the Bible, as reported by Robert Boyd.

> This Book, which we call the Bible, contains the mind of God, the State of man, the way of salvation, the doom of sinners, and the happiness of believers. Its doctrines are holy, its precepts are binding, its histories are true, and its decisions are immutable. Read it to be wise, believe it to be safe, practice it to be holy. It contains light to direct you, food to support you, and comfort to cheer you. It is the traveler's map, the pilgrim's staff, the pilot's compass, the soldier's sword, and the Christian's charter. Here paradise is restored, heaven opened, and the gates of hell disclosed. Christ is its grand subject, our good its design, and the glory of God its end. It should fill the memory, rule the heart, and guide the feet. It is a mine of wealth, a paradise of glory, and a river of pleasure. It is given you in life, will be opened at the judgment, and will be remembered forever. It involves the highest responsibilities, rewards the greatest labors, and condemns all who trifle with its content. It is the word of the living God, and is indestructible, incorruptible, indispensable, infallible and inexhaustible.[3]

21

God said to Joshua about the Bible, *"Do not let this Book of the law depart from your mouth; meditate on it day and night, so that you may be careful to do everything written in it. Then you will be prosperous and successful."* Joshua.1: 8. No other book in history has sustained the test of criticism, persecutions, and oppositions more than the Bible. Those who are opposed to it try to destroy it by different means, including trying to burn it, but it has survived.

I need this Book, you need this Book and everybody needs the Bible. Our future relies on how we consider the word of God found in the Bible.

The Bible is the heaviest and the most powerful Book there is. Here is the proof:

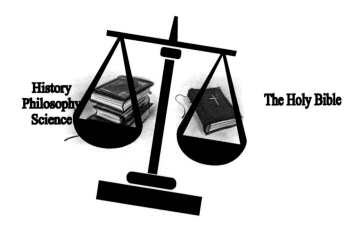

The Bible weighs more than all of these books combined.

2.   Is the Bible inspired by God?

II Peter 1:20, 21 *"Above all, you must understand that no prophecy of Scripture came about by the prophet's own interpretation. For prophecy never had its origin in the will of man, but men spoke from God as they were carried along by the Holy Spirit."* The word inspiration is translated from a compound Greek word "theopneustos" which means "God breathed." It is a theological concept encompassing phenomena in which human action, skill or utterance is immediately and extraordinarily supplied by the Spirit of God."[4]

The Bible says: *"All Scripture is God breathed and is useful for teaching, rebuking, correcting and training in righteousness, so that the man of God may be thoroughly equipped for every good work."*(II Timothy.3:16)

Should we have any doubt about God inspiring those men who wrote the Scripture, or should we listen to those who bring criticism about the way God inspired those men to write the Scripture? If we read and understand the Scripture itself, no doubt or criticism will be able to shake our belief in God and in His word. We have in the pages of the Scripture itself more than enough evidences to remove all doubt, and silence all forms of criticism.

God has prepared those men before the foundation of the world in order to use them at the proper time to write His word. In Ephesians 1:4, the Bible says: *"For He (God) chose us in Him before the creation of the world to be holy or "set apart" and blameless in His sight."*

Look at Moses. Because God chose him to write His word and to accomplish extraordinary works for Him, the Devil tried to kill him from birth by the hands of pharaoh, but God protected him so he could accomplish what God had prepared in advance for him to do. (1) Be the leader of God's people. (2) Receive the law of God for His people. (3) Write the law of God in the Bible for all the nations of the earth.

The writers of the Scripture did not bring themselves to God and say: "we want to write the Scripture." On the contrary, God said: "I have chosen you before..." God said to Isaiah by the mouth of the prophet himself: *"before I was born the Lord called me; from my birth he has made mention of my name…He who formed me in the womb to be his servant."* Isaiah 49:1,5.

To Jeremiah God said: *"before I formed you in the womb I knew you, before you were born I set you apart; I appointed you as a prophet to the nations.* Jeremiah.1: 4, 5.

Inspired by the Spirit of God, Paul said: *"The Gospel I preached is not something that man made up. I did not receive it from any man, nor was I taught it; rather I received it by revelation from Jesus Christ...God, who set me apart from birth, called me by His grace to preach Him among the Gentiles.* (Galatians 1:11-16)

So we can see clearly that, though the Bible has many authors, it conveys the same message through different men with different style. Michael C. Bere puts it this way: "Since God is the creator of language, and the master of all style, He could give His word in the style of David, Peter, Paul, Jeremiah, and thirty-six other men, and yet God's word remained God's word, just as a trumpet, a trombone, and a sousaphone, if "breathed into" by the same musician, all exhibit unique styles, so the "forty or so" writers of Scripture when inspired by God, exhibited their own personal God prepared styles when they wrote down the words that God breathed into them[5]

D.L. Moody said: "I know the Bible is inspired because it inspires me.[6]

Are you inspired by the Bible? If not, do you know why? It's because you are not yet connected to God by the person of Jesus Christ.

3. Is the Bible true?

John 17:17 *"sanctify them by your truth; for your word is the truth."* The Bible is the source of absolute **truth**, absolute **authority**, and absolute **sufficiency**.

A. If you are looking for the truth, you've just found it and it is complete. You do not have to look anymore for truth because it is in your hand in the pages of the Holy Scripture.

Jesus said: *"I am the way, the truth, and the life..."* John 14:6. When you are reading the Bible, you will always find the truth, the whole truth and nothing but the truth.

If you are honest in your thoughts, if you are a true believer, when you find the truth, the Holy Spirit will convince you to embrace it. You don't want to fool yourself, do you? If you make your own interpretation of the scripture and try to make it fit with the Bible then you are on dangerous ground and you need to come back quickly before you reach the point of no return. It would be very imprudent on your part to seek to twist the word of God in order to make it say what you want. The Bible must be interpreted by itself. The only help that is required in interpreting the Scripture is the Holy Spirit. The Bible says: *"Do not be deceived: God can not be mocked. A man reaps what he sows."* Galatians 6:7.

I believe that we should have a warning on the cover of the Bible with these words: **"Danger, handle with care!"** Perhaps that will help people think about what they have in their hands. The Bible is not an ordinary book that people can treat any way they wish. It should be treated with awe.

B. If you are looking for authority, no other person, no other book, no other authority can give you more power than the one which is available to us in the Bible, which comes from the mouth of God Himself. At creation God used that authority to bring forth everything in the universe, visible and invisible.

God just spoke the word and whatever He called came into being. *"Let there be light! And there was light."* *Genesis.1:3*

In Matthew 28:18, 19 Jesus said: *"All authority in heaven and on earth has been given to me. Therefore go and make disciples of all nations, baptizing them in the name of the Father and of the Son and of the Holy Spirit."*

The authority of the Scripture is found in the one who wrote it. So the interpretation of the Scripture must be done accordingly. If you believe that the Bible is the word of God, you must accept God's authority in interpreting it as well. Otherwise:

27

(1) You are not a true believer. (2) You cannot benefit from the word of God. (3) You cannot help others in their search for God and His authority in the Scripture. (4) You receive no authority from God. (5) You are then unable to understand and interpret the Holy Scripture.

C. If you are looking for sufficiency, you can end your search in this area, for the Bible is sufficient for whatever you are looking for. If you are always looking for something and from time to time you think that you have found it, but soon you realize that was not the case at all, I can assure you that you've now found it. Because it is in your hands right now. The Bible says in Psalm 42:1, 2, *"As the deer pants for streams of water, so my soul pants for you, oh God. My soul thirst for God, for the living God. When can I go and meet with God?"*

So the sufficiency that you are looking for is found only in God and in His word. To find it you need to: (1) Surrender your life to God. (2) Start reading the Bible regularly. (3) Pray and ask God to help you understand what you are reading. (4) Be willing to accept the word of God as is. (5) Be ready to obey all the commands of God. Then you will realize that the sufficiency you are looking for is found in the word of God.

When you read the Bible, you need to pay close attention to everything. Our God is a God of every detail. When reading a contract, you need to focus your attention especially on the fine print. God does not use fine print, but He cares for every word.

He inspired it to be written.

One lady thought that she was a victim of a health club that was withdrawing her money even after many letters of cancellation because of a medical problem. After she failed on her own to stop them from taking her money, she sought the help of an attorney. When the attorney read the contract he found in the fine print where it said that the letter must be signed by your doctor. Then the attorney suggested to her to obtain such a letter, and they immediately stopped taking her money.[7]

Do you notice what was missing? The supposedly small matter of who was required to sign the letter. The Bible is signed by God Himself. Every word counts, every dot on an "i" is important. So, watch out! Remember, the Bible is sufficient. Our addition to or subtraction from the word of God is useless if it does not say what God says. And that is why the Bible is so full of warnings against false teachers. Judgment day is coming. We all must be careful about the word of God. Both teacher and disciple will have to answer to God about what they did with His word. People who live in the USA and/or in countries with a similar system know about the I.R.S.(Internal Revenue Service). Every individual is responsible for his or her tax return. Only you will pay the consequences, not your tax return preparer.

This must remind us about the word of God. We can not blame our teachers, pastors, seminary professors, Sunday school teachers, and all the rest for our false belief regarding the Scripture. Every believer has the same responsibility that the Bereans had: Read, search, pray, seek guidance from the Holy Spirit so that you can understand and interpret the Bible the right way. As Christians, let's not fail to find and apply all the little details of the word of God. I once worked for a major electrical contractor. While working on a big project the supervisor called all the employees for a meeting. "First of all, he said, the owner wants the project to move faster. Secondly, he is willing to pay some incentives to make that happen.

Everybody is welcome to work as many hours as he wants. On top of that, every employee who works at least 60 hours in six days will receive an extra $100.00 bonus." The race was on. Almost every employee was ready to start making some serious money. The company held one week behind on pay roll. So after two weeks of work we received the first pay check with the overtime and bonus. However, a few minutes after receiving their paychecks, about half of the employees filled the office up because they did not receive the $100.00 bonus. The secretary said that there must have been a mistake.

Then they went and pulled the time cards to verify everybody's claim. Guess what? None of them was qualified to receive the bonus. Why? You may say…because they missed something that was said by the supervisor. He said: "whoever works at least sixty hours in six days will receive the bonus." But those people did work sixty or more hours, but they did so in seven days. The supervisor stated that after six days of work, you need one day to rest; if not, you can not produce enough to deserve a bonus because you are too tired."

So fellow believers, Christians, future ones, let us watch! Let us be careful with the word of God, the Bible! *"For the word of God is living and active, sharper than any two edged sword, it penetrates even to dividing soul and Spirit, joints and marrow; it judges the thoughts and attitudes of the heart."* Hebrews 4:12. The Bible can heal, but it can also hurt. It can repair, but it can also rip. In other words, the Bible is: **"Dangerous and must be handled with care."** If not, be ready to face the consequences later on!

4. Is the Bible Trustworthy?

Proverbs 3:5,6. *"Trust in the Lord with all your heart and lean not on your own understanding; in all your ways acknowledge him, and he will make your paths straight."*

The Bible is the most trustworthy book there is on the face of planet Earth. Every thing the Bible says has or will come to pass. Every prediction of God in the Bible will come to pass. All His promises will be accomplished, and all His prophecies will be fulfilled. D. James Kennedy noted that: "More than two thousand of God's prophecies have already come to pass."[8]

The best way to eliminate doubt about the Bible is to start reading it and ask God to guide you and reveal Himself to you through His word. It is unfortunate that so many people who call themselves Christians try to make the Bible what they want it to be. They choose to believe some parts of the Bible but reject other parts that are not suitable to their life style. However, as Christians, we must believe the whole Bible. The Bible is a whole, though it has many books. The Bible is absolutely trustworthy.

The New Testament is the fulfillment of the Old Testament. In the Bible God reveals Himself to man. He shows His love for man and provides a way to rescue man from his sins. From the beginning God mentioned His plan of Salvation when He said: *"I will put enmity between you and the woman, and between your offspring and hers, he will crush your head, and you will strike his heel."* Genesis.3:15.

In that passage, it is a question of Jesus Christ Himself and the church. Jesus Christ is the seed of the woman…His death on the cross crushed the head of the devil, though the devil bruised the heel of Jesus Christ. The victory over Satan was complete with Jesus' resurrection. When Jesus said: "I will build my church and the gates of Hades will not overcome it," he meant that His church on earth will continue to crush the head of Satan though Satan will continue to attack the church. But one thing is certain, victory has been won. As Christians all we have to do is to hold on to the victory given to us by Jesus Christ.

We can do that by learning the Scripture. (1) Read the Bible. (2) Pray. (3) Try to memorize one verse at a time. (4) Search the Scripture as the Bereans did. You will receive insight from God by the Holy Spirit so you can understand and apply the word of God in your life with obedience, faithfulness and diligence. I believe you have probably learned the little song which goes: "Read your Bible, pray every day, and you will grow up."

You cannot say I like this part of the Scripture, but I do not like that one. You need to pay close attention to every word and make sure to keep them.

Satan came to this world through our first parents because they were careless about the word of God. As believers, everything that the Bible requires us to do, we can and must do it. God will forgive our ignorance, but not our arrogance.

I took a Bible course some years ago where the professor was teaching about some difficult passages found in the Scripture. He said something that will help everybody who wants to know more about the Bible. He said: "The Bible is like a fish that you are eating. The fish is good, you like the fish, but it is full of dangerous bones. Do you stop eating the fish because of the bones? Of course not, rather, you take the time to remove the bones and continue to enjoy your fish. He said, this is the same thing with the Bible. There are difficult parts in the Bible, but you do not stop reading the Bible for that. You simply spend more time in studying, and in prayer, and keep reading and searching for what the Lord wants to communicate to you." My friend, do not stop, keep searching and trusting the Bible.

CHAPTER TWO

THE CREATION

1. What is Creation?

In Genesis 1:1 the Bible says: "In the beginning God created the heaven and the earth."

Though we often speak about creation in terms of fabricating, making, inventing and/or innovating, there is an extreme difference between man's creation and God's creation.

Man creates or invents something out of what God has already made. But God creates out of nothing (Ex Nihilo). "Creation is a divine act by which God called into being "heaven and earth", or all of reality out of "nothing" or without resorting to any preexisting matter." [1]

This implies that God has always been there. God was not created, but He is self-existent.

Nothing can be created by itself. R.C.Sproul said: "it is impossible for something to create itself. The concept of self-creation is a contradiction in term, a nonsense statement... Nothing can be self-created. Not even God can make Himself. For God to create Himself He would have to be before He is. Even God can't do that." [2]

Analyzing this statement will help us figure out very quickly how stupid the theory of evolution is. If man evolved from the monkey, then who created the monkey? If the monkey evolved from an inferior creature, then who created this inferior creature? And so on…this is to say that man did not evolve from another creature, but God is the maker of man and the creator of the whole universe.

The whole account of creation is found in Genesis chapter one. The Bible gives us in detail what God did every day, from the first day to the sixth, and then he rested on the seventh day. It is true that God created the world in six days and he rested on the seventh day. But I believe that God could have created the world in six hours or less, but God created everything in the way he did to teach man both the importance of work and rest. He created a pattern of work for man. There are seven days in the week. God took six days to create the universe to teach man to labor in six days, and to take one day to rest.

You might say, how do you figure that out? Very simple, (1) God did not need six days to create the universe. He could have created it in much less time. (2) God rested the seventh day. Do you think that God has ever needed a rest? The Bible says: "God is always at work." *"He who watches over Israel will neither slumber nor sleep." Psalms 121:4.*

What do you do when you want to teach your child/children to do something? Do you just tell them or do you model what you want them to do? If you want them to do it well, then modeling is the right way.

The teacher who teaches a child to write A,B,C makes the first line of A,B,C, and the child then copies what he/she sees the teacher doing.

(3) So God only gave a model of work and rest to man. This is to say that every man needs to work and to rest.

The Bible says: *"...If a man will not work, he shall not eat".*
II Thess.3:10

It also says: *"In vain you rise early and stay up late, toiling for food to eat. For he grants sleep to those he loves." Psalms 127:2.*

(4) When God created the universe, He did not need professional assistance from architects, engineers, or laborers; nor did He need any equipment like cranes, bulldozers, or any building materials or anything like that. He only used the word of His mouth. *In Psalms 33:6, the Bible says: "By the word of the Lord were the heavens made, their starry host by the breath of his mouth." In verse 9, it says: "For He spoke, and it came to be; He commanded, and it stood firm."*

In Psalms 148:5, speaking about the creatures, *the Bible says: "Let them praise the name of the Lord, for He commanded and they were created."*

In Genesis 1:3, we read: *"Let there be light," and there was light."* And so on...And everything God created accomplishes its purpose. The sun has never stopped, except in the case of Joshua's request (Joshua 10:12, 13).

No star has ever fallen on the earth-The ocean never crosses its boundaries, except in natural catastrophes like the recent tsunami in Asia and Africa. But other than that, the sea respects its boundaries. I am a witness of that; I live in the great state of Florida one of the best in the U.S.A. Most of the whole state of Florida is at sea level, but the only time we see the ocean barely pass its border is when there is a hurricane.

There is however one creature of God who refuses to do what he was created to do and this creature is, of course, man. And as a result, man's creations also fail. "The creations of man may be beautiful, but often times they do not deliver what they promise. It is not like that in heaven, for in the presence of God, there is no deception."[3]

The world was not created by chance or by accident either, but by the almighty God. Jeremy Taylor said. "What can be more foolish than to think that all this rare fabric of heaven and earth could come by chance, when all the skill of science is not able to make an oyster?"[4]

2.   Who are we?

We were not evolved from another creature, nor did we come to existence by a big bang, or by any other stupid theory. We are the work of a supreme being, called God.

After God created everything in the universe, He made man and woman to have dominion over the rest of His creation.

In Genesis 2:7, the Bible says: "And the Lord God formed man from the dust of the ground and breathed into his nostrils the breath of life, and man became a living being."

That is how man came to planet earth. God Himself made man with dirt and breathed into man's nostrils and man became a person or a living creature.

I want you to notice something in this verse.

(1) God made man; nobody else made man. (2) Man is not evolved from an inferior creature. (3) Man was made with dirt, meaning, man is nothing without the help of God. (4) Man became somebody after God put His breath in man, in other words, if you do not have God, Jesus Christ
in your life; you are incomplete. Only God can make you somebody. Do you want to be somebody? We became a "nobody" when sin came into the world by the first Adam, but there is hope for you and me through the second Adam, who is Jesus Christ. If you really want to be somebody, turn your life to Jesus Christ, your creator and savior.

From Adam and Eve to now, nobody can ever create another man or woman again. Satan was once bragging to God about his great knowledge and said that he too can create a man. God said: "Is that right? You can create a man like me…!" Satan said, "Yes, I can." God said, "I want to see that!" Then, Satan said, "Wait and see." Satan went and gathered what he needed. He took some dirt, some water, and a stick, and he said to God, "Come and see." Then he took the dirt, the water and the stick to begin his creation, when God said: "Wait a minute; first, you need to make your own dirt, your own water and your own stick, because what you have in your hand is mine." And the project stopped.[5]

This is to say that the real creator is God and Him alone. We can only imitate our creator and do our own little thing using His stuff, but we can not really create like God did.

If we are intelligent beings, we need to focus our attention on Creationism and not on Evolution. We have an account of God's creation in the Bible. We see the outcome of God's command to Adam and Eve to be fruitful, multiply, and fill the earth (Genesis.1:28). We are the proof of that. But we have never seen or heard of a monkey that became a man at anytime in human history. That means there is not one iota of proof for the theory of evolution.

The evolutionists could probably say that their proof of Evolution is a caterpillar which becomes a butterfly…However that was also part of God's creation, a procedure by which God brings a change in an organism that He has created. This is an image illustrating the change that man feels when he is reconnected to God by the new birth. *In II Cor.3:18, we read: "And we, who with unveiled faces all reflect the Lord's glory, are being transformed into his likeness with ever increasing glory, which comes from the Lord, who is Spirit."* As Christians, we need to stand for Creationism and reject the theory of Evolution. We also need to bring creationism back to every educational institution in all Christian nations of the world.

God created a perfect universe and a perfect man. When God created the world there was no mistake. Everything was in perfect order. The world became as it is today by the intervention of the devil. The word devil is from the Greek word "Diabolos" meaning divider, the one who splits asunder. So everything that we look at today that is not right in this world is due to the fact that Satan came into the Garden of Eden and messed things up. We will talk more about Satan's intervention in God's creation in another chapter.

3. What is the mission of man?

When God created man, He also had a plan, a mission for man, His favorite creature. In the making of man, God said: *"Let us make man in our image, in our likeness. Let them rule over the fish of the sea and the birds of the air, over the livestock, over all the earth, and over the creatures that move along the ground" Genesis.1:26*. Notice what God said when He was about to create man!

(1) He wanted to make man in His own image - an intelligent creature having the spirit of God in him.

(2) He wanted man to have the capacity to govern in an orderly fashion, not like how most of the governors of the world rule. The way of governing of most of the world leaders today is inspired by Satan himself, not by God.

(3) He wanted man to establish his government over all other creatures on the earth. Today when a man or a woman becomes a victim of a snake, or a bear, or a lion, it is the result of sin, thanks to Satan who seduced our first parents. God gave man authority over all His creation, but man lost that authority partially when sin entered the world.

(4) He wanted them to be fruitful and increase in number; to fill the earth and to subdue it.

Notice that God created them male and female. *In Genesis 1:27, we read: "So God created man in his own image, in the image of God He created him; male and female he created them."*

41

That means God's mission was for both, man and woman. At the age of maturity, God wants one man and one woman to be married and to reproduce so as to fill the earth with people. God never had the intention for two men or two women to co-habit as a couple. This is an abomination in the eyes of God. We will say more about that later.

4.   What is the Difference between Man and Woman?

In today's society, Satan wants to make people believe that man and woman are the same. This is a lie. We are not the same. Man and woman are equal, but different from one another.

If we were the same, God would have made us at the same time. Remember, God made the man first, and then God said: *"It is not good for man to be alone; I will make a helper suitable for him." Genesis 2:18.*

The difference between a man and a woman is as clear as crystal. If the world refuses to acknowledge that, it's up to them. However we Christians need to recognize that difference and live as God planned for us to live to please Him in everything we do. If not, we will pay dire consequences.

We are going to look at some differences that man and woman have.

(1) **Physically** we are different. The man is made to lift larger burdens than the woman. For this reason the shoulders of the man are bigger and stronger than the woman' shoulders. The

woman has bigger hips than the man. God made the woman like that for child bearing and delivery.

Just by looking at a person, you can tell if that person is a man or a woman even though he/she dresses to fake it in a movie or in other situations. The man naturally has more muscle than the woman. And the list goes on if you want to think about that. The Bible says *in I Peter 3:7 " Husbands, in the same way be considerate as you live with your wives, and treat them with respect as the weaker partner and as heirs with you of the gracious gift of life, so that nothing will hinder your prayers."*

(2) In military service God never intended for woman to become a member of the armed forces,(except for in some administrative positions). It was not God's plan for the woman to go and fight in wars. Look at what the Bible says in Deuteronomy 20:5-8:

*"...Has anyone built a new house and not yet dedicated it? Let **him** go home...Has anyone planted a vineyard and not begun to enjoy it? Let **him** go home...Has anyone become pledged to a woman and not married her? Let **him** go home...Is any man afraid or faint hearted? Let **him** go home..."*

Did you notice the frequency of the word, "**him**" but not one instance of "**her**"? Do you think God wants a woman to be a soldier? No, no, no. So a Christian woman should not become a military officer in any branch of the armed forces.

If only we take note of what prisoners of war (POW's) have endured, we would understand rather quickly that fighting in a war is not for a woman, except in rare cases where as a police officer, a member of the coast guard, or a security officer they can work with friends and family members in their own environment. They can also offer good help in the case of any national crisis or natural disaster such as a hurricane or an earthquake. Women are naturally the kind of people to assist the victims of such disasters. But women should not go to fight in any foreign war, especially Christian women. That is against God's will.

I want you to know that I am not discriminating against the woman in any form. On the contrary, I am a protector of the woman, just as God said in the Bible, in *Ephesians 5:22-25 "Wives, submit to your husbands as to the Lord. For the husband is the head of the wife as Christ is the head of the church, his body, of which he is the Savior. Now as the church submits to Christ, so also wives should submit to their husbands in everything. Husbands, love your wives, just as Christ loved the church and gave himself up for her."*

When God said to the woman to be submissive to her husband, it **was** for her own well-being. God also called for the man to be the chief of the woman, which means to be her protector, her provider, her security, her everything which is good. Notice what is said: "As Christ loves the church and gave himself for her…" Even so, the man is supposed to love

44

his wife. That means, love her enough to be ready and willing to be killed in protecting her.

The woman who does what the Bible says to do is well protected and is happy in her married life. She is not going to receive any abuse from her husband and from other people, because she is covered with the favor of God Almighty. My mom and my dad have been practicing the Bible since their childhood. My mom never received any abuse from my dad. I've never heard a curse word come out of my parents' mouths. The only time that my mom received at least some threat of abuse was when she was a little girl.

Her parents were devil worshipers. Her godfather was one also. However, her godfather by the name of Talma Dorestin became a Christian. He presented the gospel to my mom who was his goddaughter and she accepted Christ as her personal Savior when she was about 10 years old. Now when she was in her parents' house, there were some problems. So, her father and mother went to consult a Voodoo priest, and they found out that my mom was the reason for it. They tried to force my mom to recant her faith. When she would not do that she was exposed to some types of abuse…So she went and told her godfather who came to talk to her father and mother, who were his friends. Despite his attempt to lead them to receive the gospel, they refused to accept Christ and my mom would not quit believing. They worked out a compromise where my mom went to live with her godfather. As a result of worshipping Satan my mom's parents died very early. The devil killed them. My mom's godfather, though illiterate, became a powerful Evangelist through the assistance of the Holy Spirit. My mom, who did not get the chance to go to school either, started working at age fifteen for a missionary couple by the name of Vance and Joyce Brown. Pastor Brown was an American and Mrs. Brown was a Canadian. Those two missionaries went to be with the Lord some years ago, but their works did not die with them.

They were the founders of the first high school in our region. We thank God for their ministry among us and we also thank God for those who supported them and other missionaries like them. I want you to know that they brought thousands into the kingdom of God by immediate ministries and continue to bring many more into the kingdom by applying *II Timothy 2:2, which says: "And the things you have heard me say in the presence of many witnesses entrust to reliable men who will also be qualified to teach others."* I want to encourage you who are reading this book to support missions and missionaries. This is one of the best investments that you can participate in for the Lord.

My mom later married my dad, and they have five children, Daniel, Odany, Edith, Philippe and Ilene Augustin.

As women, neither my mom nor my sisters ever received any kind of abuse from my father. And this legacy goes on to us their children as well. I do not abuse my wife, or my two daughters. I believe the same is true for the wives of my two brothers and my sisters who also married two Christian men (J.Tardieu Suprien and Wilfride Michel) who fear the Lord. So they do not believe in abusing their wives and children either. I also believe that will continue from generation to generation since we pray and teach our children to choose their future partner according to the Bible's instructions. They must pray and ask God to select the right person for them to marry.

I want you to know that I am for the protection of woman, not against it. I write especially for Christian women regarding the roles of man and woman in the Biblical perspective. I want to reiterate that man and woman are equal, but different. My views are Bible based and are focused on our differences, not our equality.

(3) **In the work place-** There are jobs that are for women and other jobs that are meant for men to do. God never planned for a woman to be a construction worker. It was not God's intention for a woman to work with a sledge hammer or a pick axe or to operate a crane, and so forth…I was working for a private electrical contractor, and the supervisor who was a nice person and was willing to help, asked me: "Is your wife working?" I responded, "Not at the present time." Then, he said, "Bring her tomorrow, because we are hiring!" So I asked him, "To do what?" He answered, "to do minor electrical work, clean up debris, to do this, that, you know…!" Then I said, "Thanks for the offer, but my wife is a woman and a

47

Christian." He said, "What is that supposed to mean?" I said: "As Christians, we go by the Book." He said "What book?" I answered, "The Bible." Then he paused for a minute, and said, " I am lost; I thought I was helping you!" Then I told him, I understand that and that is why I say thanks for the offer. I know you do not know much about what I am talking about, but, let me tell you a little bit about the Bible and God...."

First, the Bible is the word of God. Second, God is the creator of the world and He also created man and woman. He created the man first and He said: "It is not good for man to be alone. So I am going to make a helpmate for man." By this word, helpmate, God meant a lot of things. God created man and woman equal but different. We both have our limitations. There are things that are woman's and things that are man's. Certain kinds of work belong to man and other kinds belong to woman. For this reason, I answered you the way I did.

My wife and I are Christians and we live in accordance with the word of God. I can work for you as an electrician, but my wife can't. If you are hiring a secretary and my wife is qualified for the position, then she can come and work for you, but, not in construction. God did not make women to carry a chip in hammer, a ban saw, an electric drill, a sheet of plywood, and all the rest. Women are not equipped to do that. I told him, not to be offended either, because you are not the first person I've said that to. I only had the opportunity to go into more details with you since we are traveling together. Then I asked him, "Do you know why today's women think they can do everything men can do and vice versa?" He said, "No, why?" I said, "Alright, I am going to give some reasons. (1) They are ignorant. (2) They do not know who they are and why they were created. (3) Because of the eighteenth century movement called "liberation of women." (In reality Jesus Christ liberated women two thousands years ago. In Galatians 3:28 the Bible says: *"There is neither Jews nor Greek, slave nor free, male nor female, for you are all one in Christ Jesus."*) *That movement did something good for the rights of women, but also caused a lot of damage to women.* (4) A lack of gallantry by men who, instead of protecting women, rather abuse them. (5) In general, the result of sin entering the world causing men and women to rebel against God and His plan for them. These are the major reasons why women do all that they are doing today."

Some professions belong to women, and some belong to man. Let's consider the medical field for instance. I believe both men and women are called to that field, but with certain particularities. Both can be medical doctors. The profession of a pediatrician fits a woman better than a man. My wife once took one of our daughters to see a doctor. For some reason, she was crying, and the doctor, who was a man, left the baby mad and said he would come back when she was quiet...I guarantee you that a woman would not have done that. At the same time, if I were to go to the hospital to have

49

surgery, I would want my surgeon to be a male, not a female. You might say why? Simple, the woman's heart is different from the man's heart. In my opinion the woman's heart is too sensitive for that kind of work. But, if I am in the hospital, I would like to have a woman as my nurse. The woman nurse has the heart, the patience to help a patient better than a male nurse.

(4) **In the Home-** What do you notice when you enter a home where there is no woman? Well, you notice that you've just entered a lifeless home, a ghost house, in some cases a cemetery. Why? Because there is no woman in the house. The furniture is not right. The kitchen is not in order. The bathrooms are in bad shape, you name it…

With regard to the care of children…Can a father take care of the children like the mother can? Does a father have the patience to feed the children like a mother does? It takes my wife about 30 seconds to change a diaper, but it takes me about 30 minutes. Our boy, **Onesiphore,** is going to be seven soon and my wife still spends a lot of time feeding him when everybody else has left the table one to two hours earlier. Can men do that? I can't! Can you? Who first notices a change in the temperature so that the children are properly dressed, the man or the woman? If you are a parent and you take your child to a child care center, and when you get there you realize that only men are working there, would you leave your child? I wouldn't. Because if you do, you may end up picking up your child in the hospital (if you're lucky) or in the funeral home (if you're not).

One more question -- how many men teachers do you see in kindergarten classes in any school? God made us like that. We both have our advantages and our limitations and we need to thank God for them and accept them as there are. Nothing and nobody can replace the patience, the tenderness, the sensitivity of a female in children's care.

(5) Have you ever noticed the difference between a man and a woman working as a bank teller and/or cashier?

If not, the next time you go to the bank or to the supermarket, stay in the line where a man is the cashier and see how much longer you are going to wait. But if you don't have all day and you want to get out quick, stay in the line where a lady is the cashier. No matter how many people are in her line, you are going to save a lot of time. Now when you go to those institutions, make sure to use some of the time that you save for the work of the kingdom.

(6) We can also notice the difference in our conduct.

Our hearts are different. The woman's heart is softer than the man's. Because of that, I believe that more women are going to go to heaven than men. They are more receptive to the gospel of Christ and they fill the church in every service. You can also check out the difference in your city by calling and asking for a report of male and female criminals who are locked up downtown.

You are going to find more than twice as many men than women are locked up. Here are a few statistics for the last five years in the State of Florida:

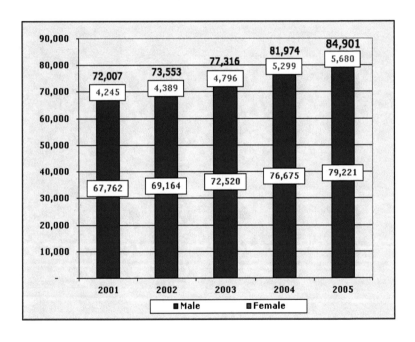

JUVENILES	Juvenile Males		Juvenile Females		Total	
	Number	Percent	Number	Percent	Number	Percent
Felonies						
Sentenced (365 days or more)	12	2.6%	1	5.9%	13	2.7%
Sentenced (364 days or less)	77	16.5%	0	0.0%	77	15.9%
Pretrial	349	74.7%	14	82.4%	363	75.0%
Awaiting Sentencing	24	5.1%	0	0.0%	24	5.0%
Misdemeanors						
Sentenced (365 days or more)	0	0.0%	0	0.0%	0	0.0%
Sentenced (364 days or less)	1	0.2%	1	5.9%	2	0.4%
Pretrial	3	0.6%	1	5.9%	4	0.8%
Awaiting Sentencing	0	0.0%	0	0.0%	0	0.0%
Minors Beyond Staff Control (HRS)	1	0.2%	0	0.0%	1	0.2%
Juvenile Subtotal	467	100.0%	17	100.0%	484	100.0%

Finally, let me add a suggestion for everybody's benefit. I hear all the time about discrimination in the work place. Some employers pay more money to the men because they supposedly work harder. In many cases, that is not true. I agree that the man is physically stronger than the woman. It was God's intention to make it that way. Many women work very hard to make up for that difference, and as a result they work even more than the men, but they still receive less salary than the men. In such a case, then, we need to start paying the women more money than the men in roles such as nurse, kindergarten school teacher, home maker, secretary, bank teller, and cashier.

Let us be honest and do the right thing. Treat everybody as they should be treated. That was God's intention when He created the world: **"Liberty, equality and justice for all."**

I mean no offense to anybody in what I write about the difference between the sexes. I base my opinion on what I find in the Bible, on past experience, on testimonies from friends and relatives, and on common sense.

5. And what's next?

Though Satan came and messed up the world, God has always had His plan to fix the world. Jesus Christ is the fulfillment of God's prepared plan for mankind. For thousand of years this plan has been worked out to reconcile man with His creator.

God calls everyone to reconciliation with Him through Jesus Christ. In II Corinthians 5:18, 19, we read: *"All this is from God, who reconciled us to himself through Christ and gave us the ministry of reconciliation: That God was reconciling the world to himself in Christ, not counting men's sin against them. And he has committed to us the message of reconciliation."*

When God created the world, he had you in mind and He is calling you now to be reconciled with Him through His Son, Jesus Christ. Are you willing to do that? I hope you are! All you have to do is to call on the name of the Lord the best way you know how. The Bible says: *"whoever calls on the name of the Lord shall be saved."* Acts 2:21

God has a lot in store for those who accept His call to come back to Him. His plan is unveiling day by day, and He is willing for you to be included. So, act now, for we do not know what tomorrow may bring. Remember that we are all God's creation, but we are not all God's children. The plan of God to restore the world is for those who become His children through Jesus Christ and not for those who remain only His creatures.

Are You A Born-Again Christian Or A So-Called One?

CHAPTER THREE

BRIEF HISTORY OF ISRAEL

1. What is the origin of the Jewish people?

There was no Israel before Abraham. The Jewish people began with Abraham, a friend of God who found favor with Him when he put his trust in the true and living God. *"Abraham believed the Lord, and he credited it to him as righteousness."* Genesis 15:6

Abraham was the son of Terah. His name was previously Abram, which means (elevated father), but God changed his name to Abraham, which means Father of a multitude. (Genesis 17:5)

In reality, Abraham became the father of many people.

A. He was the father of the Jewish people through his son Isaac, the promised son by God. (Genesis 21:1-3)

B. He was also the father of the Edomite people through Esau, the brother of Jacob. Genesis 35:29; 36:1,2.

C. He was also the father of the Arab people through his son Ishmael when he went to Agar, his Egyptian servant, following his wife's counsel, so she might have a son through her. (Genesis 16:15)

D. Abraham is also the father of the Midianite people by
another marriage with Ketura after Sara's death. (Genesis
25:1, 2.)

E. Again Abraham was given many more children after his
death in response to the promise God made to him in
Genesis 12:1-3: the Lord had said to Abraham: *"Leave
your country, your people and your father's household
and go to the land I will show you. I will make you into a
great nation and I will bless you; I will make your name
great, and you will be a blessing. I will bless those who
bless you, and whoevercurses you I will curse; and all
peoples on earth will be blessed through you."*

In other words, Abraham was also the father of all born
again Christians through Jesus Christ. In Matthew 1:1 we
read: *"A record of the genealogy of
Jesus Christ the Son of David, the Son of Abraham."* So, if
you have true saving faith in God, then you are a child of
Abraham. However, Israel, the Jewish people, is the physical
descendant of Abraham, the line by which God accomplished
the promises made to Abraham to benefit the whole world.

Abraham was indeed a man of faith. He did leave his
country as God told him to go to a land promised to him by
God. Can you imagine the pressure that Abraham might have
been under by his family and friends?

Some might have told him: "Abraham, you see what you
have, but you don't know what you are going to receive…

58

Maybe you are suffering from depression. Abraham, why don't you go to see a psychologist? You are leaving all your relatives behind you to go to an imaginary place nobody knows where! This is crazy, Abraham!"

However, in spite of all the objections Abraham might have encountered, he did proceed to go in the direction of the country that God promised to him. Not too many people can do that! The difference was that Abraham believed God with all his heart. Do you believe God like that?

God did, in fact, keep his promise to Abraham and he gave the land, as promised. Our God is a trustworthy God.

God gave Abraham a fourfold blessing because of his unaltered faith in Him. God gave him:

(1) "A personal blessing- A great name was promised to him.
(2) A land blessing- A great country was promised to his descendants.
(3) A national blessing- Promise of a great nation.
(4) A spiritual blessing- promise of favor of God which will reach all the nations through Abraham's posterity."[2]

Abraham also demonstrated his faith in God when he was willing to sacrifice his son, the one he had when he was 99 years old and his wife was 90 years old, because God had asked him to do so. How much faith do you have in God? Through that son Abraham was promised a great posterity, but by faith he was going to offer that precious son to God because he had faith that God would bring him back to life again. In fact, God spared Isaac's life altogether when he brought forth a ram for Abraham to sacrifice in the place of Isaac.

Isaac became the father of twins, Esau and Jacob. God chose Jacob, but rejected Esau. So the promise went from Abraham to his descendant. In Jacob, the grandson of Abraham, God formed the twelve tribes of Israel, who at a certain time went to Egypt because of famine in Canaan. There, God developed the nation of Israel under the leadership of one of them, Joseph, the beloved son of Jacob. Joseph left his father's house to serve his brothers who in turn sold him as a slave to some slave merchants.

They in turn resold him to Potiphar. After being falsely accused by Potiphar's wife, he went to prison for about two years. After about thirteen years of unjust suffering, God raised him up as the prime minister of Egypt. In all the hardships that Joseph had been through, God was preparing him for that position. God used the gift that he gave Joseph to interpret dreams, to bring him to the second position in a foreign land.

My friend, are you suffering hardships, trials, or difficulties of some kind? Well, God may be working in you to prepare you for something special. I urge you to be patient, take heart, pray to God; ask him to give you strength to endure all until you are fully prepared for what God has for you.

2. Why did God choose the Jewish people?

Man chooses differently from God. Man usually chooses the biggest, the strongest, the mightiest because man helps and brings assistance. However, God chooses otherwise. He did not choose the Israelites because they were the biggest or the strongest; rather they were the smallest among the nations. "The Lord did not set his affection on you and choose you because you were more numerous than other peoples, for you were the fewest of all peoples."(Deuteronomy 7:7)

God chose the Israelites people because: (1) He loved them. (2) He kept His promises made to Abraham in their behalf. (3) To make them a Kingdom of priests and a holy nation.

"But it was because the Lord loved you and kept the oath he swore to your forefathers that he brought you out with a mighty hand and redeemed you..." (Deuteronomy 7:8)

In Exodus 19:6, we read: "You will be for me a kingdom of priests and a holy nation..."Because Abraham did not reject the call of God, he was loved by God and received all kinds of blessings from God for himself and for all his descendants, physically and spiritually.

61

As Abraham was a source of blessings to many; are you a source of blessings to other people also? If not, it may be because you are not a real child of Abraham.

Do you know that the same way God chose the Jewish people, He chooses us also? He loves us. He showed His love to us through Jesus Christ. He has promised to save us if we believe in His Son, Jesus Christ. He will make us His servants. Think about that!

3. What is the plan of God for the Jewish people?

God wanted to make them into a great nation. However that would not happen overnight, nor would it be easy. God promised Abraham to make a great nation of his descendants, but they would first be slaves in a foreign country, and after 400 years He would bring them back to the Promised Land.

Genesis 15:13: "Then the Lord said to him, know for certain that your descendants will be strangers in a country not their own, and they will be enslaved and mistreated for four hundred years."

Joseph was the first to go to Egypt as a slave. Then his brothers went some years later because of famine in the land of Canaan. God arranged it that way so they would meet the brother they hated. Though they did not recognize him the first time, the second time he revealed himself to them. He was a type of Jesus Christ. The same thing happened to the Jewish people at Jesus' first coming. Many of them did not recognize him as the Messiah. As a result, Joseph's father Jacob and the whole family came to Egypt triumphantly since Joseph was the man in charge of all Egypt next to king Pharaoh. The number of persons who came to Egypt with Jacob was seventy. They lived in peace in the land of Goshen. (Genesis 45:10)

The Israelite people multiplied greatly and filled the land of Egypt. Then there came a king who did not know about Joseph; he called the Egyptians and told them: Look these foreigners are become much more numerous than us. If there is a war and they join to our enemies and fight against us...! We must do something...!

First, the Egyptians made them slaves and oppressed them with forced labor.

Second, they killed all the male babies among them to keep them from being so many.

However, after 400 years, God visited His people because he wanted to accomplish His promises in their behalf.

4. God chose a deliverer.

I do not know what you are going through right now. But I can tell you that if you are a child of God, he cares about you the same way that he cared about the Israelite people.

In Exodus the third chapter, God attracted Moses' attention to a bush on fire, but the bush was not burned up. God called Moses, gave him His command to stop and remove his sandals from his feet because he stood on holy ground, then God told him that:

" I am the God of your father, the God of Abraham, the God of Isaac and the God of Jacob...I have indeed seen the misery of my people in Egypt. I have heard them crying out because of their slave drivers, and I am concerned about their suffering. So I have come down to rescue them from the land of the Egyptians and, to bring them up out of that land into a good and spacious land, a land flowing with milk and honey... " Exodus 3:6-8

I want you to notice four wonderful things that God did for His people.

(1) I have indeed seen the misery of my people in Egypt

(2) I have heard their crying.

(3) I am concerned about their sufferings.

(4) I have come down to rescue them from the land of slavery to transport them into the best land there is. Beloved, do you know that the God of the Israelite people is the same God that we Christians serve

today? Do you know that God sees you where you are? Do you know that He hears your prayers, and that He is working in your situation right now? Do you know that God is concerned about your problems, sufferings, misery, sickness, and so on? And best of all, He does not sit down and do nothing about it. On the contrary, He is willing to help, to assist you, to deliver you and prepare you to come to a land where there is milk and honey. God is always ready to send a Moses in our life to deliver us from our misery. Isn't that wonderful!

In spite of the many objections of Moses, he had to go fulfill God's command anyway. Pharaoh tried to resist the commands of the Lord, but no one in the Universe can successfully resist the commands of the Lord. In Isaiah 46:10, 11 the Bible says: *"I make known the end from the beginning, from ancient time, what is still to come. I say: my purpose will stand, and I will do all that I please. From the east I summon a bird of prey; from a far-off land, a man to fulfill my purpose. What I have said, that will I bring about; what I have planned, that I will do."*

My friend, my brother, my sister, no one can successfully resist the will of God. Moses could not. Pharaoh could not. Jonah could not. You and I cannot either. God uses everybody as He wills.

65

Satan is God's servant when God gives him the order. God can use every one of His creatures if He wants to. He used a donkey to rebuke Balaam (Numbers 22:22-35). He ordered ravens to feed Elijah (I Kings 17:2-4). He sometimes uses a thorn to keep a Christian humbled, like in the case of Paul, the apostle (II Corinthians 12:5-10). When Pharaoh was playing big shot with God, God used the ten plagues to show Pharaoh that He is God, and that there is none other after Him (Exodus 7-11). Pharaoh resisted God during the first nine plagues; but when God decided to put an end to it, He told Moses: "Get ready, you, the people and everything that belongs to them because in the middle of the night Pharaoh will push you out of Egypt."

5.   The Passover.

When the time had come for God to free His people, He gave the order to Moses and Aaron to tell the people what to do, and to get ready because their departure was drawing nigh. They were to kill a lamb and apply the blood on the sides and tops of the doorframes of their houses where they were to eat the lamb with certain regulations.
Everyone who wanted to be rescued obeyed the commands of Moses and did as they were ordered to.

God was about to strike Egypt with the tenth plague. Everyone who did not apply the blood would suffer the lost of their first born (Exodus 12).

So, the Lord almighty brought His judgment to the land of Egypt and brought His people out of slavery with his mighty hand. So God sent the angel of death to strike every first born of Egypt from people to animals, and in the middle of the night, as God had said, Pharaoh called for Moses to tell him: "Take your people and go…" In Isaiah 14:24 we read: *"The Lord almighty has sworn, surely, as I have planned, so it will be, and as I have purposed, so it will stand."*

Yes, the same night the people of God were free to go. By the powerful hand of God they left the land of Egypt, the land of slavery, to head toward the promise land. It was not without difficulties, for we all know what happened right in front of the Red Sea, when Pharaoh and his army decided to go after the Israelite people. But also we cannot forget what God did for His people. He delivered His people from the danger of the Red Sea by opening a dry road right in the middle of the sea. The only difficulty that the people of God had in the middle of the sea was dust, because it was too dry in the just created road, while the Egyptian's army drowned by the waters of the Red Sea. What an awesome God we have!

67

Everything was provided for the children of Israel. Water when they needed it; bread, manna and meat when they were hungry. Light and shade were provided for them by the Shekinah (the cloud of God). Rest was also given to them when they were tired. A house of worship was built as the center for God's adoration. First, the Tabernacle as a mobile house of worship with the Ark of Covenant symbolized God's presence among His people and second, the Temple of Jerusalem. God promised to meet with His people in His Temple.

6.   The Ten Commandments.

And the best of all was the Ten Commandments that God gave His people on Mount Sinai through Moses as intermediary, His special servant, to teach them how to live to please a Holy God.

Here are the Ten Commandments. Exodus 20:1-17

And God spoke all these words:
I am the Lord your God, who brought you out of
Egypt, out of the land of slavery.
You shall have no other gods before me.

You shall not make for yourself an idol in the form
of anything in heaven above or on the earth beneath
or in the waters below.

You shall not bow down to them or worship them;
for I, the Lord your God, am a jealous God,
punishing the children for the sin of the fathers to
the third and fourth generation of those who hate
me, But showing love to a thousand generations of
those who love me and keep my commandments.

You shall not misuse the name of the Lord your
God, for the Lord will not hold anyone guiltless who
misuses his name.

Remember the Sabbath day by keeping it holy.
Six days you shall labor and do all your work,
But the seventh day is a Sabbath to the Lord your
God. On it you shall not do any work, neither you,
not your son or daughter, nor your manservant or
maidservant, nor your animals, nor the alien within
your gates.

For in six days the Lord made the heavens and the
earth, the sea, and all that is in them, but he rested
on the seventh day. Therefore the Lord blessed the
Sabbath day and made it holy.

Honor your father and your mother, so that you
may live long in the land the Lord your God is
giving you.

You shall not murder.

You shall not commit adultery.

You shall not steal.

You shall not give false testimony against your neighbor.

You shall not covet your neighbor's house. You shall not covet your neighbor's wife, or his manservant or maidservant, his ox or donkey, or anything that belongs to your neighbor.

7. The Ultimate Sin of the People of Israel

While Moses went before God on Mount Sinai to receive the law of God for the people, they fell into idolatry. They asked for a god that they could see. They demanded it from Aaron who in turn agreed to commit such an abomination in the eyes of God by making a golden calf for the Israelite people to worship (Exodus 32). How many leaders today are just like Aaron? They are doing the will of the people that they serve instead of honoring God as their highest priority!

If you are a leader, watch out! What happened to Aaron and the people of Israel can still happen to you today. God is the same in every generation.

8. The First Generation Forbidden to enter the Promised Land

The Israelite people tried God many times, and God forgave them every time by the intervention of Moses. However, by continuing in sin, they exhausted the patience of God. God expressed this in these words to Moses: "Nine times they have insulted me by not putting their trust in me, now for the tenth time they are still insulting me. For this reason, none of the old generation will enter the Promised Land." Do you know what causes the wrath of God to overflow? It is the result of the influence of **bad leaders**. Ten spies who did not trust God, but looked at what they saw. When the two good leaders tried to help the people to understand the power of God, they attempted to stone them.

But, one thing remains: God has spoken. Go back to the desert until you, the old generation, are all dead. **This took forty years.** The Israelites could have reached the Promised Land in **one week**, but because of unbelief, it took them **forty years**...And only the new generation went in, the ones who were not old enough to have seen and understood the wonders of God in getting His people out of Egypt. Beloved, do you trust the Lord? Or do you only say that you trust Him? (Numbers 13:26-33; 14:1-25)

9. The Two Special *Ones*

Only two men from the old generation were allowed to enter the Promised Land.
Joshua and Caleb found favor with God to enter the land because they put their complete trust in the Lord. They did not waver in their faith. God honored this kind of faith, and he will prove himself faithful to anyone with such a faith.
In the same way **that faith in God took** Joshua and Caleb into the **Promised Land,** faith in Jesus Christ will take a person to **heaven.**

10. Leaders, beware!

Moses and Aaron did not enter the Promised Land because of a minor infraction, for something considered as a misdemeanor in the USA, meriting as punishment only community service.

Aaron let the people lead him into idolatry, and he joined Miriam in gossiping about Moses.

Moses himself struck a rock that God had told him to talk to, in order to provide water for the people. Although Moses was angry because of the people, that did not give him an excuse for disobeying God.

Are you aware of how harsh your judgment will be as leaders? Moses pled with the Lord to forgive him and let him enter the land, but

God told him the best He could do for him was to let him go to the Mountain and look at the land, but not put his feet on it. So Moses died on Mount Nebo and Joshua became the new leader who would bring the people to the Promised Land.

11. The leadership of Joshua and the conquest of Canaan

A) The Call of Joshua

God called Joshua and said: *"...Moses my servant is dead, now then, you and all these people, get ready to cross the Jordan River into the land I am about to give to them to the Israelites."* Joshua 1:2

In verses 6-9, God gave seven specific commands: *"(1) Be strong and courageous. (2) Be strong and very courageous. (3) Be careful to obey all the law my servant Moses gave you. (4) Do not turn from it to the right or to the left that you may be successful wherever you go. (5) Do not let this book of the law depart from your mouth.*

(6) Meditate on it day and night, so that you may be careful to do everything written in it. (7) Do not be terrified, nor be discouraged, for the Lord your God will be with you wherever you go."

Joshua became the new leader of the people of God. He was a man under authority, and others received his authority as well. God was with Joshua as he was with Moses. The sign of the Red Sea was repeated in the crossing of the Jordan River. This news melted the hearts of the people in the land of Canaan. They were very afraid.

B) The Circumcision of the New Generation.

The sign of the Covenant God gave Abraham was very important. They could not go to possess the land without the circumcision of every male among the people of Israel. Do you remember what had happened to Moses when he was on his way to Egypt? He had not circumcised one of his sons, and for this God almost killed him. His wife Zipporah had to do it for him. Today many Christians think that they do not need to be baptized... How wrong they are! There is a lay preacher by the name of Ernst Leon in a church where I was a member. He used to say this: "If you say that you are a Christian and refuse to be baptized, whatever is stopping you from being baptized can also stop you from going to heaven." Jesus wants every Christian to identify himself with Him in baptism. Beloved, don't be negligent, do what is important to identify yourself with Jesus Christ.

C) The fall of Jericho- Possession of the Promised Land.

Jericho was the mighty city, which had scared the ten spies sent by Moses and caused the old generation to condemn themselves to death in the wilderness when they refused to honor God for the tenth time.

Joshua and his army were near Jericho when Jesus Christ showed up with His drawn sword in His hand. When Joshua questioned Him, saying: "Are you with us or against us?" He identified Himself as the commander of the army of the Lord and He gave command to Joshua, who obeyed immediately. With Christ's appearance to lead and empower the people of Israel, the stronghold city of Jericho became history. How obedient are we to the commands of the Lord? Do you know that many strongholds and fortresses are still standing before us for the simple reason that we do not receive and obey the commands of the Lord?

Israel was victorious as long as they followed the commands of the Lord. They failed at Aï because they sinned. Acan stole devoted items. They were also tricked by the Gabaonites, because Joshua failed to consult the Lord. The roadblocks in our lives could be many things, but the most important of all is the neglect to follow the commands of the Lord in whatever we do. If Jesus Christ is our master, we must act as His slaves!

Joshua warned the people of God's wrath if they were to abandon Him. He also told them that as for himself and his household, they would serve the Lord.

12. The New Leaders of Israel- The Judges, The Kings and The Prophets

After the death of Joshua, the Israelite people became very idolatrous. On many occasions, God gave them up to their enemies, but because of His covenant with Abraham, Isaac and Jacob, He also provided deliverers for them. The judges were their next leaders for many years. There were two kinds of judges.

1. "One was a magistrate in charge of judging civilian matters when there was a dispute or a crime of some kind. This began with the counsel of Jethro to his son-in-law, Moses. Moses took too much

responsibility on himself and Jethro advised him to delegate power to wise, courageous, and faithful men so he could lighten his burden by only taking on the more difficult matters. (Exodus 18:13-26). Moses told the Israelites to establish judges when they arrived and were living in the Promised Land (Deuteronomy 16:18-20).

2. The other kind of judge was a man called by God to lead an uprising of the people of Israel against a foreign oppressor. When such a judge brought liberation to the people, it was a sign that God was with him, and he became the defender of the people. There were twelve of those liberator judges from Othniel to Samson."[3] (Judges chapter 3 to chapter 13).

After that came the kings, for Israel rejected God as their king, and asked for a king that they could see. Samuel, a prophet and spiritual leader, told them what God said, that it would not be in their interests to have such a king. But they would not listen. So God gave them such a king.

The first human king of Israel was Saul, the son of Kis, from the tribe of Benjamin. During his forty years as king, Saul proved numerous times his spirit of disobedience to the Lord and so God chose a replacement. David became the kind of king that God would choose for His people. David was succeeded by his son Solomon, then Solomon by his son Rehoboam during whose reign Israel became two kingdoms. Judah became the kingdom of the south, and Israel, the kingdom of the North with Jeroboam as king. "They were 20 Kings who reigned from Rehoboam to Sedesias in the southern kingdom, which is Judah. They were 19 Kings who reigned from Jeroboam to Hosea over the northern kingdom, which is Israel."[4]

Many prophets fulfilled their ministries to the kings and to the people of Israel. There were both true and false prophets. The true prophets were sent by God Himself, and the false prophets were self proclaimed, sent by the Devil.

The well-being of the people depended on their leaders. When their leaders were persons who feared God, the country was peaceful and prosperous. They listened and followed the guidance of God's prophets. But when their leaders did not fear God, the country was desolated by wars, and eventually the people went into captivity. The false prophets led the bad leaders into making bad decisions, which in turn brought down the curse of God on his people. However, God never broke His promises made with their forefathers.

13.   The Extension of the Kingdom of David.

After the failure of the human kings, God still promised to send a descendant of David, as promised, to restore the kingdom of David. The promise was made in II Samuel 7:16: *"... Your house and your kingdom will endure forever before me; your throne will be established forever."* After Malachi, the last Old Testament book, God was silent for four hundred years. But, because of his promises, he had to do something. He then caused the last Old Testament prophet by the name of John the Baptist to prepare the way of the Lord.

After John fulfilled his ministry, God took him away and the Savior of the world, the Messiah, the Christ, the Son of Man came as the promised one of Israel to accomplish the promises of God made to Abraham, Isaac and Jacob.

14. The Mistake of the Jewish people- The Benefit of the Gentiles.

- Jesus Christ is the Messiah.

Most of the Israelites failed to recognize their Messiah. Yet, the Gentiles received Him, and millions of them are being saved. In John 1:11, 12, we read: *"He came to that which was his own, but his own did not receive him. Yet to all who received him, to those who believe in his name, he gave the right to become children of God."* Jesus Christ, though he was fully God, came as a man through the Virgin Mary, grew up, was baptized, fulfilled His earthly ministry, died on the cross for the sin of the world, and rose the third day from the grave according to the scriptures. After forty days of giving instructions to His disciples, He went back to heaven, where He had come from.
By this, Jesus Christ brought to an end the dispensation of the law and began the dispensation of grace or of the church, which was born ten days after His ascension.
(Acts 2)

Beloved, whether you are Jewish or Gentile, there is only one way of Salvation: Jesus Christ is the way. Have you surrendered your life to Him? If not, would you like to do so now? Just say, Jesus, please save me. I surrender my life to you now...In Jesus' name, Amen!

CHAPTER FOUR

THE TRIUNE GOD

1. Is there a God?

Throughout the history of mankind, people have been asking this question: "Is there a God?"

The French philosopher Voltaire said: "If there were no God, they should invent one!" But he also messed it up when he said: "If there is one, they should abolish Him!" I want you to forget the second part of his thoughts and focus on the first one. God is so indispensable that if there were no God, they should really invent one. I don't know if you remember the true meaning of invent…it means to find. In order for you to find someone or something, he or it must have been already there. "Many voices proclaim the existence of God: the voice of creation, of conscience, of history, of philosophy, and the voice of the life of Jesus Christ. God has also revealed Himself."[1]

We are all on the earth today because there is a God who created us. Now it is our responsibility to find Him.

C.S. Lewis was an atheist until he came to his senses and asked himself the question: "How do I know that something is wrong? He said that man does not say that a line is curved unless he has an idea of what a straight line is. To what do I compare this universe when I say that it is unjust?"[2] Just as Lewis did, good reasoning will help you discover God.

God said: *"You will seek me and find me when you seek me with all your heart."* Jeremiah 29:13. According to the Bible, only a fool can say that there is no God. In Psalms 14:1, we find these words: *"The fool says in his heart, there is no God."* Maybe a very small percentage of the world's population repeats such foolishness, but when a large percentage of people act like there is no God, they are on the same side with those who say that there is no God.

If you are an individual who questions the reality of God, I want to reassure you that there is a God. The Bible is the most reliable book there is, and it is the word of the living God. God speaks to us throughout the scripture to make Himself known to us.

God created Adam and Eve. He revealed Himself to many individuals in the Bible. One of the persons He revealed Himself to was Noah. When the earth was so corrupt and full of violence and God decided to destroy it, He spoke with Noah saying: *" I am going to put an end to all people, for the earth is filled with violence because of them...So make yourself an ark of cypress wood...* "Genesis 6:11-13."

God also revealed Himself to Abraham. In Genesis chapter 12, God spoke to Abraham and made some great promises to him, which came to pass. God also revealed Himself to Moses in Exodus 3, when He sent Moses to Egypt to rescue His people from bondage. When Moses inquired as to who was speaking to him through the burning bush, God answered in verse 6 saying: *"I am the God of your father, the God of Abraham, the God of Isaac and the God of Jacob..."*

When Moses was skeptical and asked God, "Suppose I go to the Israelites and say to them, the God of your fathers has sent me to you, and they ask me, what is his name? What shall I tell them?" *God said to Moses: "I am who I am."* Exodus 3:13,14

My friend, there is a God. God is real and you can find God if you set your heart to look for Him.

2. There is one God in three Persons.

This is what we call the triune God or the trinity. It is true that some people object to the idea of a triune God, but that does not eliminate the reality of a God in three persons. The doctrine of Trinity appears all over the pages of the Holy Scriptures. Genesis 1:1 says: *"In the beginning God created the heavens and the earth."* The Hebrew word for God, "Elohim" is a plural, which allows for and foreshadows the fuller revelation in the New Testament of the three persons. In Genesis 11:7, we find also the trinity implied in the story of God investigating man's project to build a great tower that would touch the heavens. The Lord said: *"Come, **let us go** down and confuse their language so they will not understand each other."*

Also in the Bible in miniature, which is Isaiah 6:8, we read: *" then I heard the voice of the Lord saying, "whom shall I send? And who will **go for us?** "* In the New Testament right before Jesus began His earthly ministry, there was a manifestation of the trinity at His baptism. In Matthew 3:16,17, the Bible says:

"As soon as Jesus was baptized, He went up out of the water; at that moment the heaven was opened and he saw the spirit of God descending like a dove and lighting on Him. And a voice from heaven said, "this is my Son, whom I love; with Him I am well pleased."

Look my friend, though this is a quote from the Bible, you don't have to accept it as it is; go and read it for yourself in the Bible.

We find almost a repetition of that manifestation also in Matthew 17:2-5. It was at the transfiguration when Moses and Elijah were talking to Jesus. The Holy Ghost appeared that time in the form of a bright cloud, and the Father spoke again to identify the Son, the one He loves. Also when Jesus gave the great commission to His disciples, He said in Matthew 28:19 *" Therefore go and make disciples of all nations, baptizing them in the name of the Father and of the Son and of the Holy Spirit,"*

We also find the presence of the triune God in the Epistles. In I Corinthians 12:4-6, Paul said: *"there are different kinds of gifts, but the same spirit (Holy Spirit), different kinds of service, but the same Lord (Jesus Christ). There are different kinds of working, but the same God (the Father) works all of them in all men."*

Beloved, it is true that the word trinity is not found in the Bible, but the Holy Book is saturated with the doctrine of trinity. The only thing that will prevent you from recognizing this doctrine in the Holy Scripture is a lack of true faith in God.

When you put your faith completely in Jesus Christ, you will have eyes opened to the reality of God as one God in three persons.

3. Where is God?

God is everywhere. Two of the attributes of God are His immanence (meaning that God is close to us) and His transcendence (meaning that God is far from us).

Though God's throne is in the third heaven, he is unlimited in His presence, His knowledge and His power. In Psalms 33:13,14, we read: *"From heaven the Lord looks down and sees all mankind; from his dwelling place he watches all who live on earth."*

In Psalms 66:7, it is said: *"He (God) rules forever by His power, His eyes watch the nations, let not the rebellious rise up against him."*

"For He (God) views the end of the earth and sees everything under the heavens." Job 28:24

In Proverbs 15:3, the Bible says: *"The eyes of the Lord are everywhere, keeping watch on the wicked and the good."* Have you ever noticed the presence and reality of God? In Psalms 19:1, the Bible says: *"The heaven declare the glory of God, the skies proclaim the works of His hand."*

The incredibly complex organization of the universe speaks about a supreme being. And that being is no one else but God Himself. People can choose to ignore that there is a God. They can act as if there is no God. But they cannot prove that there is no God, since the evidences of God are everywhere. (1) Look at yourself and consider how you could have come to existence without a supreme being? (2) Look at the ocean and ask yourself why it does not overflow the land? (3) Look at the stars, the moon and the Sun that have never stopped giving light. The stars have never fallen on anybody or caused damage to any country. (4) There has never been a breakdown in any of the stars or in the galaxies. (5) Have you ever gone out at night and lifted up your eyes to look at the heavens? (6) Have you ever watched the coming of the rain? (7) Have you ever observed the wind? These are just a few of the wonders of the world, which only God could have created.

So, if you are not a fool, you cannot say that there is no God. And if you have an iota of wisdom you will not repeat such a foolish and dangerous statement.

Now it's up to you to find God. If after observing all these things, you are still unable to realize that there is a God, then I encourage you to look for where you belong as being either in the vegetable or the animal kingdom. You do not have the ability to use your five senses, you have no vision, no intelligence, you are deaf, and you have stopped being a human.

And the only way you can become one again is by confessing your sin of unbelief. Stop being a rebel. Surrender to your creator. Acknowledge Him, and He will rescue you because of His great love for you, for your family members, for your friends and for the world.

My friend, God is near you, He is in heaven, and He is everywhere.

4. Where did God come from?

When I was in high school, I was privileged to go to a Christian institution. My Bible teacher by the name of Reverend Evince Plancher was once talking about God, and a student asked the question: "Where did God come from?" Pastor Evince said: "God has no beginning and no end. He has always been." But the student persisted in his quest for a more definite answer…then the teacher said: "My friend, if you don't want to lose your mind, accept what every body else has accepted from the Bible about God. He has no beginning, and no end. He has always been. He is eternal…"

Maybe you have been asking the same question for sometime now…

The answer is the same from the pages of the scripture. In Isaiah 43:10 we read: *"…that I am he, before me no god was formed, nor will there be one after me. I, even I, am the Lord, and apart from me there is no savior."* In Isaiah 45:5, we read: *"I am the Lord, and there is no other; apart from me there is no God…"*

Also in Isaiah 46:9, 10 we read: *"….I am God, and there is no other; I am God, there is none like me. I make known the end from the beginning, from ancient time, what is still to come. I say: My purpose will stand. I will do all that I please."*

Do you get it, my beloved? This is the eternal God speaking. He is God from everlasting to everlasting. Stacy Robinson, a professional football player, said in his testimony: "three things will last for ever: (1) God, (2) God's word, and (3) and God's people.[3]

My friend, nobody can answer this question to your satisfaction before you establish a relationship with God through His Son Jesus Christ. Look, if you were to ask Jesus Christ this question, He would answer you the same way. Do you remember in Jesus' ministry when He was talking about Abraham in John 8:56-59. *"....Your father Abraham rejoiced at the thought of seeing my day; he saw it and was glad. And the Jews said to him: You are not yet fifty years old, and you have seen Abraham! Jesus said: I tell you the truth, before Abraham was born, I am. At this, they picked up stones to stone him..."* Do you **understand** the declaration of Jesus to the Jews of His time?

He said: "I am Eternal. I have no beginning and no end. I have always been." But the people wanted to kill him for blasphemy.

There are only three witnesses of God. (1) God, the father. (2) God, the Son. (3) and God, the Holy Spirit. There was a devoted Haitian Christian lady by the name of Mrs. Maurice Celestin (who now lives in New York) that my wife is always telling me about. When some people walked in her house to talk about the gospel, at first she received them joyfully. When they were seated, she then asked them: "Who are you? What is your denomination?" When they answered: "We are Jehovah's Witnesses. Then she said: "Oh, I have a question for you! Who is the father of God, and who is His mother?" And it was like the end of the conversation. They understood that this was not somebody that they could persuade to abandon her belief. She was a member of an evangelical church with sound doctrine.

I use this as an illustration to show you once more that God has no eyewitnesses of His existence other than the three persons of the trinity.

I have nothing against the Jehovah's Witnesses sect either. I only hope and pray that they will soon come to accept the doctrine of Trinity and recognize the deity of the Holy Spirit and of Jesus Christ, and accept Him as Lord and Savior.

My friend, all you need to know about God is revealed in the Bible, and what you need to accept that revelation is faith in the Lord Jesus Christ. When you put all your trust in Him, then you will be satisfied with what is made known to you in the word of God. In Deuteronomy 29:29 we find a wonderful verse that can help you on this matter. It says: *"The secrets things belong to the Lord our God, but the things revealed belong to us and to our children forever..."*

We also read in I Corinthians 13:9, *"for we know in part and we prophesy in part, but when perfection comes, the imperfect disappears."*

Believe in the Lord Jesus now. Learn all you can by the assistance of the Holy Spirit and the teachers in your church; read the Bible, pray, and when it comes to the mysteries of God, accept them for what there are. When the time comes for us to know perfectly, then God will certainly reveal these things to us.

Are You A Born-Again Christian Or A So-Called One?

CHAPTER FIVE

THE FALL OF MAN

1. What is Sin?

It is unfortunate but a reality that for many sin is defined today only as acts such as murder, adultery and robbery.

Today, lying is not a sin for many, since in their opinion, there is no absolute truth. The meaning of disobedience today is a matter of personal opinion, because what is disobedience for me is not necessarily the same thing for others. We live in the age of absolute irresponsibility. Do as you wish; as long as you can justify it, it is not a sin. I was in a bank sitting down waiting to be served when a young lady walked in and sat on a chair next to me. She began a conversation with me. While we were talking, she dropped her cell phone. When she picked it up and was observing it for damage, she said: "If my phone breaks I am going to sue…" I said: "Whom are you going to sue?" She said: "The bank!" I said: "Look, you dropped your phone because you did not hold on to it well enough and you think you can sue somebody for your negligence!" she said: "I did not drop it, gravity did…" And guess what, I not only believe that she would sue, but I also believe that she would find some lawyer who would argue such a case for her.

Beloved, this is to tell you that many people are experts in making arguments. They know how to argue a case and how to defend themselves. But **God's definition of sin remains the same.**

Sin is breaking God's law. Anytime you and I disobey God's law, we sin. We are not the ones who define sin. God is the one who does so, because in order for somebody to define sin adequately, such an individual must be perfect. The reason why many of us can define sin today is the fact that we have learned it from the word of God.

In other words, what people in general consider as sin is not accurate. Murder, adultery, robbery are just a fraction of all the different kinds of sins there are.

There are different categories of sins and there are hundreds, if not thousands of sins. We sin in words, in actions, in thoughts, with our eyes, with our ears, with our hands and with our feet.

Do you remember singing a "chorus" when you were a child, maybe in Sunday School, saying: "Be careful little eyes what you are watching…ears what you're hearing…hands what you're touching…feet where you are going because God is in heaven watching over you on earth…" We also sin by what we do that we should not do, and by what we should do and do not do.

2. Who is a sinner?

Adam and Eve were our first parents. They were the first to sin by being disobedient to God's word. However, we are all sinners also. We have a tendency to blame Adam and Eve for what happened, but let me tell you that you and I are not better than they were. We would do worst than them, and we prove it by how far, how progressive we are in sinning. In Adam's time you had to use a weapon and stand face to face with another man in order to kill him, but now you can just release a little gas or drop one bomb and kill millions.

Therefore, we are all sinners. The Bible is clear on that. In Romans 3:23, we read: *"For all have sinned and fall short of the glory of God."*

In Romans 3:10, the Bible declares that; *"....There is no one righteous, not even one."*

Jews and Gentiles, black and white, men and women, adults and children, Europeans and Americans, Africans and Asians, and Arabs, we are all sinners.

Adam failed the test of God when the Devil came and tempted him to disobey his creator and we all failed with him. We inherit a sinful nature from Adam and Eve, and we continue to sin daily. However, God has made a plan of rescue available to all men and through His son Jesus Christ. We will study that more profoundly in the next chapter.

My friend, you may be trying hard to live a good or even a perfect life here below, but let me remind you that you are a sinner in need of a Savior. The only one I can recommend as a savior from sin is the Lord Jesus Christ. He is the only cure for sin. D.L. Moody said: "Looking at the wound of sin will never save anyone. What you must do is look at the remedy." [1]

3. What are the consequences of Sin?

We may be the generation that sins the most since the beginning of the world and we are the most prideful generation as well. We are doing what is against the will of God and we ignore God's warning, but when the consequences of our sin come we are mad with people who remind us about them.

One major problem with this generation is that most of us are allergic to the truth. The previous generations were sinners also, but they were more open to the truth. They were more humble when receiving a warning about their behavior. They either repented or tried to hide the wrong they were doing.

Today, it is the contrary. Today's generation is arrogant. People sin and displease the Lord in all kinds of ways. When you warn them, they laugh at you, but when the consequences come and you remind them, guess what? They want to hurt you worst than Herod treated John the Baptist.

This generation is trying to intimidate the true preachers of the Gospel into keeping their mouths shut, if possible. But let me tell you something, it is easier to shut the mouth of a lion with your bare hands than to silence a preacher of the word of God or the Gospel who has truly been called by the Lord.

There is a saying in Haiti which goes like this: "If you call the Devil father, he will eat you up. If you call him Satan, he will still eat you up. So, just call him "Stupid Devil.""

The meaning of this saying is this: it's not a question of who you are or what you say, but a question of who they are, unrepentant sinners. Oswald Chambers said: "Sin enough and you will soon be unconscious of sin.[2]

Sin always has consequences. If you were to ask King Saul of Israel about the consequences of sin, he would tell you that they are terrible. If you were to ask Eli, the priest, he would only murmur. If you were to ask King David, he would say, you don't want to know. God did not make the consequences of sin secret either when he placed Adam and Eve in the beautiful Garden in Eden. He told them openly if they disobeyed His commands, they would face terrible consequences, including death.

When Adam and Eve sinned, they experienced the results of their sin; the glory of God, which covered them before, departed from them. They had to hide from the Lord's presence and this separation from God is spiritual death. This is exactly what God had told them: If you eat from the tree of the knowledge of good and evil you will surely die. In Genesis 2:16, we read: *"And the Lord God commanded the man, you are free to eat from any tree in the garden; but you must not eat from the tree of the knowledge of good and evil, for when you eat of it you will surely die."*

In Genesis 3:1-7, Satan came and gave them another version and they listened to the voice of the evil one and fell into his trap and sinned against God, which brought chaos on the face of the planet for every creature. And, my friend, guess what?

Some of us are still vulnerable to falling into sin the same way. You say, how? I am going to tell you how.

(1) We think that we are smarter than God.

(2) We make our own doctrine…we remove what is inconvenient to us from the word of God to make it fit our lifestyle.

(3) We favor preachers who preach what we want to hear, not what the gospel says.

(4) We are quick to reject teachings from the Bible, saying that it is only the personal interpretation of the preacher.

(5) We sometimes accept what is pleasing to us in the gospel and reject what is not.

(6) We appreciate the cheap gospel and reject the real one.

(7) We become lovers of formalism.

(8) We make our own program to serve God and we reject God's commands on how we are to worship Him.

(9) Our churches become centers for marketing and not places to worship

(10) We dress up like people who are going to disco and bars and clubs, and we pretend to be going to church.

(11) When the preacher says something that we don't want to hear, we not only reject it, but we make sure we tell our neighbors to reject it also.

(12) We become the generation that best fits the description Paul gave in II Timothy 3:2-7. Listen to it:

"People will be lovers of themselves, lovers of money, boastful, proud, abusive, disobedient to their parents, ungrateful, unholy, without love, unforgiving, slanderous, without self-control, brutal, not lovers of good, treacherous, rash, conceited, lovers of pleasure rather than lovers of God, having a form of godliness but denying its power...loaded down with sin and swayed by all kinds of evil desires, always learning but never able to acknowledge the truth."

Beloved, when we act like that, we open the door to the Devil to do to us what he did to Adam and Eve and we will pay some dire consequences as well. What God said to them did happen, and God's warning to us will come to pass unless we repent. Notice what happened to Adam and Eve when they disobeyed God's commands: they died. Death comes in three dimensions, which are:

(1) Spiritual death.

That happened automatically when they sinned. They were disconnected from God, their creator. Separation took place. They became miserable. They hid from God. Do you know that we are all separated from God also? But the good news is, we are now reconnected to Him through His Son, Jesus Christ, and you can be also.

(2) Physical death.

The reason why we've never had the opportunity to meet Adam and Eve is the fact that they are dead because they sinned against their creator. And the reason why many of us are now without our husband, wife, children or parents, our friends, our co-workers, our employers, our neighbors, and so on, is because sin entered the world via Adam and Eve. Not only do we miss all these people, but we also are going down the same path, because most of us, if not all, are going to die as well.

(3) Eternal death.

Adam and Eve escaped eternal death because they agreed to wear the clothes God made from the skins of the sheep to cover their nakedness; God's action in Genesis 3:21 was a representation of the sacrifice of Jesus Christ.

You and I can also escape eternal death by means of the new birth.

We all died in Adam, but we can also live again in Jesus Christ. If you are not born again, do you want to experience that now? Just confess your sins, turn from them and invite Jesus Christ into your life, and he will save you.

4. Does God love the sinner?

Many people reject the gospel and those who preach it for the simple reason that they think that they are undeserving of the love of God. They think that they sin too much. They believe that they have already gotten too far away. They cannot come back. God will not accept them anymore...

Let me suggest something to you, especially if you are reading this book and you don't know the Lord yet, and you are thinking like this.

Do you remember or have you heard about the Prodigal Son whom Jesus talked about in the Gospel of Luke, chapter 15:11-31?

In that parable Jesus taught about a son that was lost because of his own rebellion just like you and me. He went his way like you and I do. He did bad things like you and I do. He tried to stay away from his mean father just like you and I do. He came to experience great needs like you and I have. Then he came to his senses, something that you and I sometimes refuse to do. He said to himself:" I have a plan. I know that everything I need is in my father's house. His servants are better off than me. So, here is what I am going to do:

(1) I am going back to my father's house.
(2) I am going to confess my sins to my father and to God.
(3) I do not deserve to be treated as his son anymore.
(4) I am willing to be just one of his hired servants.
(5) He started right away to go back.

And guess what? He was warmly received by his father, not as a hired man, but as a son who was lost, but then found.

My beloved, don't you think that this would happen to you also?

The key in returning to God is humility. The son humbled himself and went back and was well received. The same will happen to you if you do as he did.

This is to let you know that **God hates sin, but He loves sinners.**

If you are not in God's arms right now, it is not because of your sins, but because you refuse to abandon them and come back to God.

God is still waiting for you with His arms opened. All you have to do is to humble yourself, change your ways, return and **go** back to Him, and He will receive you.

As proof of the love of God for the sinner, He sent His one and only son to die for you and me so we can be rescued by His sacrifice.

My friend, if you are an unrepentant sinner, He is calling you right now. Do you want to come? I hope you do before it is too late. I encourage you not to wait until the last minute so that what happened to the ten virgins does not happen to you also. Rather do it now. Be ready so that whenever the call comes for you, you can respond, saying, "Here I am, Lord."

5. What will happen to the unrepentant sinner?

My friend, I don't know how many of you were victims of what I am going to describe, but I know for sure that some of you were.

When I was in primary and even secondary school, sometimes I got punished for what somebody else did. Has that ever happened to you? One kid in your class said something but the teacher did not see who the kid was and nobody wanted to snitch on the perpetrator by saying that it was "John"…! So the teacher said: "If I do not find the person, the whole class is going to write 1000 times: 'I must learn to control my mouth in the class room'." This is due tomorrow. And guess what? Everybody had to do it.

Do you know, my friend, this punishment was intended only for the kid who did something bad, but since we all aligned ourselves with him, we all had to pay.

In the same manner, my friend, God prepared a place for Satan and his angels, but if we refuse to repent of our sins, if we do not listen to the call of God, if we keep on rejecting the sacrifice of His Son, and if we exhaust His patience, then we are going to pay the same price with Satan and his angels. The place of punishment that God prepared for them will become also our place.

And that place is not nice; it is a place of suffering. It's called hell. It is a terrible place. It is a place of torment. It is total separation from God.

My friend, I don't think that you want to go to that place... And God does not want you to go there either. However, when God created man, He gave man a free will that makes man able to choose what he wants to do and what he does not want to do, because He did not want to make man a robot. And since man has a will, he can decide to obey God or to disobey Him. Although there are consequences to pay; today man can choose to obey God and surrender his life to Jesus Christ or to live as he wishes outside the commands of God.

God chose Jesus Christ, His Son, to be the basis for His judgment. If you put your trust in Him and in His sacrifice, then you are saved and are going to heaven with God, but if you refuse Him and His sacrifice you automatically choose Satan, and you are going to hell with Satan. Now this is your choice. You cannot blame God if you end up in hell, because He made provision in His Son Jesus Christ for you not to go there. But when you reject His Son, then you are on your own and you are headed to a place called hell, a place of suffering and total separation from God.

If you are without Christ, you are spiritually dead, but you will personally experience the horror of this spiritual death when you die physically.

The Bible says: *"just as man is destined to die once, and after that to face judgment."* Hebrews 9:27

So after physical death, my friend, you will face judgment. That means your real you is not going to be extinguished at physical death. Your spirit and soul are eternal. They came from God and will never be annihilated. After physical death, it is not all over. You will either live again with Jesus Christ in paradise or exist with Satan in hell. So now is the time to decide what you want to do and where you want to live after you leave the earth. The Bible declares that: "Now is the time of salvation." Do not put it off for another day, for you know not what a day may bring forth. Procrastination is a sin, and in some cases it might be deadly.

Remember, God's word is the truth, and Satan is a liar. So, listen to God. Don't listen to what Satan has to say because his words are deception and lies. And if you go to hell with Satan, you will not be able to ever come back from hell. You will be there forever and ever in suffering for all eternity. I hope and pray that you act intelligently and quickly to secure your eternity with Jesus Christ before it is too late.

CHAPTER SIX

THE DEATH OF JESUS CHRIST

1. Why did Jesus have to die?

When I was a teenager, I was listening to a Christian radio station and the host said something that attracted my attention and my dad's attention as well. My dad commented on it and that made me think even more when my dad said: "This is powerful and people need to think about it."

I believe that you want to know what the host said, don't you?

Here it is, he said: "It is okay, it's normal for people to die, but what is abnormal is when you see somebody being buried and you know that you are responsible for that person's death...!" After the fall of man, death became a normal thing. God spoke of this to Adam and Eve: "If you eat from that particular tree, you shall surely die." They did eat, so they died, and death is being passed on, on to everybody since then. Spiritual death became universal when our first parents sinned against God. However, anybody who is born of the spirit becomes alive again.

Eternal death is optional for every human being. If you are born again, you are exempt from eternal death, but if not, you will be eternally damned.

- Physical death is what we want to focus on. We ask the question: "Why did Jesus have to die?" Do you remember what the radio host said?

"It is okay for people to die, but it is not okay when you know that you are the one responsible for the person's death."

Do you know that you and I, and the whole world, are the reason for Jesus' death? Isaiah 53:5 says: "but he was pierced for our transgressions, he was crushed for our iniquities; the punishment that brought us peace was upon him, and by his wounds we are healed." You say what? But, yes, it is the case.

In John 3:16, we read: *"for God so loved the world that He gave His one and only son, that whoever believes in Him shall not perish but have eternal life."*

In Romans 5:8 we read: "but God demonstrates His own love for us in this: while we were still sinners, Christ died for us."

Beloved, have you ever thought about that? Have you ever realized that the blood of Jesus Christ was shed because of you? And now that you know that, if you did not know it before, what are you going to do to clear your name from such a mess?

You know that I am not an attorney, but I think that your best defense is to plead guilty…! If you do, God's mercy will cover you and the blood of Jesus Christ will clean you from all guilt. But if you choose otherwise, you will be condemned for life or in reality for everlasting death. Jesus Christ himself was not guilty of anything. Three times He was found innocent before Pontius Pilate. In John 18: 38b Pilate said: *"I find no basis for the charge against him."* In John 19:4, Pilate said to the Jews, "look I am bringing him out to you to let you know that I find no basis for a charge against him." And in John 19:6, as soon as the chief priest and their officials saw him, they shouted, "Crucify! Crucify!" But Pilate answered, "You take him and crucify him. As for me, I find no basis for a charge against him."

My friend, do you realize that Jesus Christ was innocent? He died for you. So, do you want to give your heart to him now? If you mean business, repeat this prayer and put your complete trust in Jesus for everlasting life.

"Dear Jesus, I am guilty before God and I come to you for mercy. Please, forgive my sins and make me a new person. I want to live to please you from this day forth. In Jesus' name I pray. Amen."

2. Did Jesus give His life deliberately or did someone force Him to do so?

Do you recall a story in the Bible where God rejected an offering offered to Him by Cain and at the same time accepted another one offered to Him by Abel (Genesis 4:1-5)?

Also, do you remember the case of Ananias and Sapphira in Acts 5, where they brought an offering to the church but God rejected it as well? And not only that, but they paid the consequences of their lack of respect for God with their own lives.

Most people have a mistaken idea about the offer of God to us because of the way the world does business. When we exchange a car in a car dealership to buy a new one, the buyer usually loses and the dealer wins, money wise.

When we receive an offer to refinance our homes, the mortgage company always portrays us as the beneficiary of big savings, but we know that they offer to us the pennies that we save because they are making the dollars.

So, we are not comfortable in the world of affairs when we consider our vulnerability to lose, especially if we think about the "**Enron scandal**" which left millions of people hung, most of them senior citizens…!

In a sense, we have good grounds to be doubtful. However, there is one difference and it is big. We are dealing with two different characters. One of them is man, and the other one is God. Man changes, but God never changes. Man is fallible but God is infallible. Man can not be completely trusted, but God is completely trustworthy.

In Numbers 23:19, the Bible says: *"God is not a man, that He should lie, nor a son of man, that He should change His mind."*

In Isaiah 55:8-9, the Bible says: *"for my thoughts are not your thoughts, neither are your ways my ways, declares the Lord. As the heavens are higher than the earth, so are my ways higher than your ways and my thoughts than your thoughts."*

In Hebrews 6:18, the Bible says: *"It is impossible for God to lie."*

In II Corinthians 9:7, the Bible says: *"Each man should give what he has decided in his heart to give, not reluctantly or under compulsion, for God loves a cheerful giver."* You might say, I don't get it…but don't worry, you will. I want to tell you:

(1) God is not a Hypocrite.

(2) God always has the right motive in giving or in anything He does.

(3) God is the most generous giver who has ever existed.

(4) God does not have any fine print in His contracts.

(5) God is the guarantor of His contracts.

(6) God's dividends are not based on the performance of any market, or economy.

(7) All God's investments are guaranteed thirty, sixty, or even a hundred times more than what was sown or invested. So, there is no possibility of loss whatsoever in the promises of God.

When God gives, He gives deliberately. The counsel of God decided to save the world. God the Father, God the Son, and God the Holy Spirit decided by one accord that Jesus Christ would come to pay the penalty of our sins. And so it was done. Listen to the words of Jesus Himself recorded in John 10:17, 18. *"The reason my Father loves me is that I lay down my life-only to take it up again. No one takes it from me, but I lay it down of my own accord. I have authority to lay it down and authority to take it up again. This command I received from my Father."*

Jesus gave His life voluntarily to save mankind. No one forced Him to. And this is the example that you and I need to follow. When we give, we must give deliberately, with the right motive, generously, and most important we must give ourselves first to God, so that our offerings may be the best that they can be. God expects His children to be like Him. Those of us who really trust God will always bring the best offerings to Him, but those who are playing with themselves, thinking that they are playing with God, always bring leftovers to God.

My friend, make a note of that, God never accepts leftovers from anybody.

Before God receives your offerings, He checks your heart first. Though often one criticizes those who judge others' motives, still we would not accept offerings from a non-believer in our church inasmuch as we have control over it. In Exodus 25:2 God asked His beloved servant Moses to collect an offering for Him from His people to build the tabernacle. He said: "Tell the Israelites to bring me an offering. You are to receive the offering for me from each man **whose heart** prompts him to give."

Dear friend, when you give, make sure that your heart prompts you to give. Give like your Father who is in heaven gives, and your reward will be great.

3. What is the effect of Jesus' death?

Many people see no positive benefit in somebody's death. Meanwhile, many will come to know God because of someone else's courage in death. Death is very powerful when the reason for dying is a noble one. Do you remember the young girl in Colorado (Rachel Scott) who died because she believed in God? And not only the mere fact that she believed, but the courage she showed when she came face to face with death. The enemy asked her the question: "Do you believe in God?" With a gun pointed to her head, she answered positively and straightforwardly…and that made a difference and brought many to the knowledge of the Savior Jesus Christ right at the funeral.

(1) Jesus' death is the reason why we have B.C. (before Christ) and A.D. (in the year of the Lord)

(2) His death reshapes the course of History.

(3) His death makes it possible for man to reestablish a relationship with God.

(4) His death brings reconciliation to God and man.

(5) His death allows us to distinguish between two categories of people on earth: a) the just, and b) the wicked.

(6) His death gives man a choice either to spend eternity with God in paradise or with Satan in hell.

(7) His death brings pardon to the worst sinner there is.

(8) His death frees man from the judgment of God.

(9) Because of His death, millions are today called children of God, or born-again Christians.

(10) His death and resurrection guarantee our victory also over death. Beloved, do you see anything negative in Jesus' death? The only thing negative I can see in Jesus' death is the fact that Adam and Eve missed the mark and that caused Jesus to suffer unto death to redeem us. But, since that had already happened, and someone had to reverse the spiritual disaster caused by Satan, Jesus came and did it. To me, the death of Jesus Christ was the most wonderful thing that could have ever happened for mankind. All we have to do is to say that we are sorry that our Lord had to suffer so much for us, but we are glad that He agreed to do it for our sake, and we love you, we thank you and we vow to serve you all the days of our lives.

My friends, the effect of Jesus' death is life for everyone who desires it. Jesus said in John 10:10 *"...I have come that they may have life, and have it to the full."*

4. Was the death of Jesus Christ sufficient to pay for the penalty of sin?

In Hebrews 8:7, we read: *"For if there had been nothing wrong with that first covenant, no place would have been sought for another."*

We also read in chapter 7:11 *"If perfection could have been attained through the Levitical priesthood (for on the basis of it the law was given to the people), why was there still need for another priest to come, one in the order of Melchizedek, not in the order of Aaron?"*

"There are (8) **eight** great covenants in the Bible.

(1) The covenant in Eden. (Genesis 2:16). That covenant had to do with the life of man in the state of innocence.
(2) The covenant with Adam (Genesis 3:15). It defined the conditions of life of sinful man and it also promised a redeemer.
(3) The covenant with Noah (Genesis 9:16). It established the principle for human government.

(4) The covenant with Abram (Genesis 12:2). It is the
foundation of the nation of Israel and in addition brought
more precision about the redemptive promise made to Adam.

(5) The covenant of Sinai (Exodus 19:5). It stated "all men are
sinners."(Romans 3:23)

(6) The covenant with Israel for the Promised Land
(Deuteronomy 30:3), which guarantees the final restoration of
Israel and their conversion.

(7) The covenant with David (II Samuel 7:16). That covenant
established the royal line of the family of David through
which Christ would come (Matthew 1:1). The everlasting
sovereignty of David's family over Israel and over the whole
earth will find its accomplishment in Christ and by Christ
Himself. (II Samuel 7:8-17; Luke 1:31-33).

(8) The New Covenant. (Hebrews 8:8). That covenant is
founded on the sacrifice of Christ and guarantees the eternal
happiness of the redeemed. That covenant is absolute. It is
definite and cannot be revoked."[1]

The two covenants mentioned in Hebrews 7 and 8 are the first or old covenant, and the new or last covenant.

If the first one was fine, perfect, we would not need a new one. In the covenant of **Sinai**; when the law of God was given to Moses for the people of Israel, God gave instructions for the people on how to live socially, morally, and religiously. There was also a special provision on how the people could worship God. Priesthood was established

with Aaron, the brother of Moses, the first priest. That office was
reserved for Aaron and his descendants only (Numbers 3:1-13)

The high priests offered thousands of sacrifices for the people and
for themselves to God, but that was not enough to cleanse their sins. It
was simply a symbol, a call to remind them of the perfect sacrifice that
would take place one day.

That is why we find these words saying: "If there was nothing
wrong with the first covenant, there would be no need for another one."

The good news is that now the new and definitive covenant, the one
that cannot be replaced, has been established. This one is complete,
whereas the first one could only cover sins, but could not erase them.
But the new covenant cleanses from and erases sins and makes the
person, by the blood of Jesus Christ, brand new like Christ Himself, not
because we become sinless, but because God looks at us through the
blood of Jesus Christ. Since the New Covenant is founded on the
sacrifice of Christ, and the sacrifice of Christ is the perfect one, the
death of Christ is therefore sufficient to pay for the penalty of all sins
for all men who so desire this salvation.

It was not possible for the blood of animals to cleanse the sins of
men. It could only cover them until the blood of the Lamb of God
came to make them totally clean. I am going to make it as clear as
crystal so that you can understand it. Suppose your dog vomits on your
kitchen floor. You say to one of your children, go and take some dirt
and cover this vomit so that I can not see it; would that clean it up? I
think not. You won't see it because it is covered with dirt, but when
somebody steps on it, you will still smell it. On the contrary, if you ask

your child to take water, soap and a mop or a rag, the mess will be cleaned up completely with no mark or smell left behind.

The same difference is seen in the result of the sacrifices of animals in the old covenant as compared to the perfect sacrifice of Jesus Christ in the new covenant.

My friend, whether you are black, white, yellow, whether you are American, European, Asian, African, Arab, whether you are Jewish, Muslim, Buddhist, Hindu, or whether you a Christian in name only, no matter what your religion is, the news that I have for you is that the sacrifice of Jesus Christ can wash your sins away and make you brand new in God's sight. In I John 1:7, the Bible says: *"and the blood of Jesus, his son, purifies us from **all** sin."* In Hebrews 7:25, 27, we read: *"Therefore he is able to save **completely** those who come to God through him, because he always lives to intercede for them. Unlike the high priests, he does not need to offer sacrifices day after day, first for his own sins, and then for the sins of the people. He sacrificed for their sins once for all when he offered himself."*

Beloved, if you are not yet covered by the blood of Jesus Christ, you are facing a great danger. You have a deadly virus in your veins right now that makes you spiritually dead and can kill you physically and eternally. Your only chance is to acknowledge that now and seek coverage under the blood of the Lamb of God, Jesus Christ, and you will be spared.

Do you want to do that? Just say, Lord Jesus, thank you for your precious blood. I am sick to death, but I want to be washed by your blood. Please, wash me with this blood of yours and save me for your blood's sake. In your name I pray. Amen!

Are You A Born-Again Christian Or A So-Called One?

CHAPTER SEVEN

SALVATION

1. What is Salvation?

Salvation is the principal word that encompasses the effects of redemption. Salvation involves rescuing someone from a danger or delivering from some kind of evil. Only people who are in danger need salvation. People who live in Florida should have a clear idea about the meaning of salvation because of the many lakes in the state. It is a common practice for citizens to help rescue people who accidentally drive or fall into the lakes. So, their understanding of rescuing others or being rescued by somebody else is an almost everyday occurrence. My wife told me about a lady who was supposedly in danger when she was having a baby in a hospital in Montreal, Canada. She was in labor and the gynecologist was checking on his patients and giving instructions to the nurses on duty regarding each patient.

Meanwhile, the doctor entered a room where a lady was apparently in pain, but when she saw the doctor, she said: "Docteur, mon dos me fait mal!" meaning "Doctor, my back hurts..!" Then the doctor said to the nurse: "Don't worry about her, because she is not yet in pain." You might say why? "Simple," he explained: "She is Haitian and she is speaking French, supposedly feeling that she is in danger"…The doctor who was also Haitian said: "When you are in real danger, or real pain, you do not speak a foreign language with your own people, you speak your maternal language."

Obviously, later on when she had real pains, she screamed: "Doctè do-m ap kasé," meaning: "My back is breaking apart," except this time, she said it in her maternal language. This time the doctor gave the order to help her right away, because she was ready.

Do you understand that? Salvation is available to you, but only if you realize that you are in real danger.

Beloved, the whole world is in danger. It is as if every man, woman, and child had fallen into a huge and deep ocean and everybody is in danger of drowning. But God, in His mercy, takes millions of life saving vests and drops them in the ocean and tells every person who wants to be saved to wear one of these vests. Now, your desire and determination to be saved will be shown when you take one of these vests and put it on you so you can be saved. Anyone who refuses to put on one of the vests proves that he/she rejects the salvation of God, thinking that they can swim well enough to save themselves. Of course, in reality, all those trying to save themselves will drown.

Jesus Christ is the life vest sent by God to rescue you and me from the huge ocean of sin. His name "Yeshua" means salvation. God announced it in Genesis 3:15 *"And I will put enmity between you and the woman, and between your offspring and hers."*

In Habakkuk 3:13, 19, He said: *"You came out to deliver your people, to save your anointed one. You crushed the leader of the land of wickedness; you stripped him from head to foot. The Sovereign Lord is my strength; he makes my feet like the feet of a deer, He enables me to go on the heights."* In Zechariah, He said: *"Rejoice greatly, O Daughter of Zion! Shout, Daughter of Jerusalem! See, your king comes to you, righteous and having salvation..."* (Zechariah 9:9). Isaiah 61:1-2 says: *"The spirit of the sovereign Lord is on me, because the Lord has anointed me to preach good news to the poor. He has sent me to bind up the brokenhearted, to proclaim freedom for the captives and release from darkness for the prisoners, to proclaim the year of the Lord's favor and the day of vengeance of our God to comfort all who mourn."*

Jeremiah 33:6 says, speaking of the restoration of God's people: *"I will bring health and healing to it; I will heal my people and will let them enjoy abundant peace and security."* Jesus is the one who does that and continues to do it for every person who so chooses.

Are you in real danger? If you do not have Jesus Christ as your personal Savior, yes, you are in real danger. And you have the obligation to do something about it. A.W. Tozer said: "Salvation is...bringing back to normal the creator-creature relation."[1] Three aspects of salvation can be distinguished:

(1) **Past Salvation**. The believer has been saved from the guilt and the condemnation of sin. II Timothy 1:9, 10 *"God has saved us and called us to a holy life- not because of anything we have done but because of his own purpose and grace. This grace was given us in Christ Jesus before the beginning of time, but it has now been revealed through the appearing of our Savior, Christ Jesus..."*

115

(2) **Present Salvation**. He is saved continually from the habits and the bondage of sin. Galatians 2:20, *"I have been crucified with Christ, and I no longer live, but Christ lives in me..."* Romans 6:14, *"For sin shall not be your master, because you are not under law, but under grace."*

(3) **Future Salvation**. He will, one day, be saved from the presence of sin, and will be perfectly conformed to the image of Christ. I Peter 1:5, *"...Through faith you are shielded by God's power until the coming of the salvation that is ready to be revealed in the last time."*

In I John 3:2, we read: *"Dear friends, now we are children of God, and what we will be has not yet been made known. But we know that when he appears, we shall be like him, for we shall see him as he is."*

This concept of Salvation is also called by Theologians:
-Predestination , which is Past Salvation
-Vocation and Justification , which is Present Salvation
-Glorification, which is Future Salvation.

2. Who can be Saved?

In Luke 19:10, Jesus said: *"For the Son of Man came to seek and to save what was lost..."*

Anybody who acknowledges his/her dangerous situation can be saved. Salvation is offered to all mankind. Whatever your origin, race, position, education, or social situation, you can be saved. If you know that you are lost, you can be saved. In Acts 17:30, 31, the Bible says: *"In the past, God overlooked such ignorance, but now he commands all people everywhere to repent. For He has set a day when he will judge the world with justice by the man he has appointed. He has given proof of this to all men by raising him from the dead."*

In I Timothy 2:3, 4, we read: *"this is good, and pleases God our Savior, who wants all men to be saved and to come to a knowledge of the truth."*

Any person can be saved, because salvation is a free gift that God offers to all men, Jews or Gentiles. However, only one person can give you salvation. His name is Jesus Christ of Nazareth. When we were in great danger, He is the one that God, the Father, sent to rescue us. It is said in Acts 4:12, *"Salvation is found in no one else, for there is no other name under heaven given to men by which we must be saved."*

Now you know that you can be saved, if you are not yet saved. Do you want to do something about it? The Bible says: *"whoever calls upon the name of the Lord shall be saved."* (Acts 2:21)

3. How can People be saved?

There are laws and regulations in every domain of life. It is the same for salvation. You cannot be saved by choosing your own means of salvation. Salvation is not something you receive from birth, nor something you inherit. Salvation is designed by God Himself. So He set the rules and regulations for salvation. We can choose to follow His directions and be saved or reject them and be lost. Salvation is by what Martin Luther called: "Sola gratia- Sola Fide –**by grace and faith**

117

only;" which perfectly harmonizes with his "sola Scriptura" **by scripture only.** We read in Ephesians 2:8 *"For it is by grace you have been saved, through faith and this not from yourselves, it is the gift of God."*

(1) Recognizing that you are a sinner, and you are separated from God.

(2) Showing your willingness to repent from your sins by confessing them to Jesus Christ.

(3) Inviting Jesus Christ by faith to enter your life and make you a new creation.

(4) Promising to live not for yourself, but for your new master.

(5) Acknowledging that it is by the grace of God that you are saved, not of your own merit.

(6) Surrendering your life under the command of Jesus Christ in everything you do.

(7) Trying to live a life pleasing to the Lord all the days of your life.

Let me illustrate that for you in this manner. Suppose by accident or by "Unbelief" (disregarding the advice of others to take precautions), you fall into a well. Now that you are 12 to 15 feet in the hole, can you give instructions to people on how to rescue you, or are you willing to listen and do as you are told to do?

The choice is yours…do as you are told and be delivered from the danger, or keep talking in vain and remain in the hole -- **which** one do you prefer? My friend, it is the same with God. You and I are in danger. God realizes that and so He sends a rescuer to save us from the danger. We must follow all His instructions if we want to be rescued.

If we don't, we are going to remain in the hole, and die there.
Beloved, many people in local churches are doing just that.

What is your intention, your motive to question the word of God?
Are you looking for more illumination to better obey the Holy
Scripture, or are you looking for a way to continue to sin?

In Jeremiah 17:10, God says: *"I the Lord search the heart and
examine the mind, to reward a man according to his conduct,
according to what his deeds deserve."*

Remember that God is the creator, and you are a creature!

4. Are you Saved?

I meet many people to whom I ask this question: "Are you saved?"
Not just like that. But I begin a conversation and before long I
technically ask the question, "Are you saved?" It became easier for me
to ask this question after I took a course on Evangelism Explosion,
founded by
Dr. D. James Kennedy, in Fort Lauderdale, Florida. (By the way, I
recommend this course to everybody who wants to be more effective in
the presentation of the Gospel of Jesus Christ.)

When I ask people if they are saved, I receive several different
answers:

(1) One of the most common answers I encounter is: "I am trying,
    I do not harm anybody…I try to keep the Ten
    Commandments.

(2) The next one is: I will not know until I die…but I do my best.

(3) The less common answer is: "Yes, I am saved by the grace of God." Hearing this answer, I say," Praise the Lord!"

My friend, since salvation is freely offered to you by God Himself, all you have to do is to accept it. Let me help you get rid of some illusions.

- You do not have to work for your salvation. You can never work enough to earn salvation.

- You cannot struggle enough for your salvation. Even if you become a world champion in your wrestling, God is not an emotional being who would be so moved by your efforts that He would grant you salvation for that reason.

- The Ten Commandments can not give salvation to any individual. Moses, who received them from God, was saved by the grace of God.

- No amount of money can buy you salvation. We sing a song in French saying: "Je suis sauvé, non pas de l'argent. Je suis sauvé non pas de l'or" meaning: "I am saved, not because of money. I am saved, not because of gold, but redeemed by the blood of Jesus, Divine ransom of His love."[2] This is what we find also *in* I Peter 1:18, 19, *"For you know that it was not with perishable things such as silver or gold that we were redeemed...but with the precious blood of Christ, a lamb without blemish or defect."*
Charles Haddon Spurgeon said: "One might better try to sail the Atlantic in a paper boat them to get to heaven in good works."[3]

So my friend, stop trying, stop being self-righteous, stop struggling, stop working, stop applying money toward your salvation. Why?

Because all these things are useless. None of them can bring salvation to you. You are saved only by accepting the free gift of God, who is His Son, the Lord Jesus Christ as your personal Lord and Savior by faith.

When you do that sincerely, with all your heart, then you accept the grace of God and you are saved. In Acts 16:31 it says, *"Believe in the Lord Jesus, and you will be Saved, you and your household."* After being saved, the Bible then requires us to work out our salvation, not for our salvation.

Faith is the most important element that you need to have in order to be saved. The Bible says: *"without faith it is impossible to please God, because anyone who comes to Him must believe that He exists and that He rewards those who earnestly seek Him." Hebrews 11:6*

Remember that salvation is a free gift from God and that only in Jesus Christ you can find it. The most important element to help you accept salvation is faith.

You and I never see Jesus Christ, or God the Father, but when we put our faith in the word of God, we can feel the presence of God, experience the power of the Holy Spirit, and realize the protection of the blood of Jesus Christ in our lives.

5. Can you lose your Salvation after you have been saved?

I meet so many people who oppose me for holding this biblical doctrine that if I did not have a solid foundation in the Holy Spirit, I would have been intimidated into not speaking of it. But, thanks be to

God, I do not back down from the truth and that is why I am still preaching the eternal security of the born again Christian. The Bible says that the person who truly believes in Jesus Christ has eternal life. He/she is eternally secure.

In John 3:16, we read: *"for God so loved the world that he gave his one and only Son, that whoever believes in him shall not perish, but have eternal life."*

In John 3:36, we read: *"Whoever believes in the Son has eternal life, but whoever rejects the Son will not see life, for God's wrath remains on him."*

In John 5;24, we find these words: *"I tell you the truth, whoever hears my word and believes him who sent me has eternal life and will not be condemned; he has crossed over from death to life."*

Also, we find in I John 5:10 to 13: *"Anyone who believes in the Son of God has this testimony in his heart. Anyone who does not believe God has made Him out to be a liar, because he has not believed the testimony God has given about His Son. And this is the testimony: God has given us eternal life, and this life is in his Son. He who has the Son has life; he who does not have the Son of God does not have life.*

I write these things to you who believe in the name of the Son of God so that you may know that you have eternal life." Based on the word of God, you **cannot** lose your salvation. If you are lost, it is because you were never saved to begin with.

Some people argue that you can lose your salvation and base this idea on the fact that Judas Iscariot lost his salvation. This shows the ignorance of the people who teach such a doctrine. Judas was **never saved.**

Jesus Christ said to His disciples: *"Have I not chosen you, the twelve? Yet one of you is a devil or demon."* *(He meant Judas, the son of Simon Iscariot)*. John 6:70.

Can a demon be saved?

If a demon can be saved, then Satan can be saved also! On the other hand, if a demon cannot be saved, then Judas could never be saved since Jesus said that he was a demon. Judas Iscariot was added to the other disciples for a reason, only to hand Jesus over to his enemies. He was hired to betray our Lord. He was never born again.

There are those who said: *"Only he who stands firm to the end will be saved."* Matthew 24:13.

The fact is the true believer, the born again Christian who lives in the word of God, will stand to the end no matter what.

However, the Bible also speaks about some carnal Christians who might not stand in the face of persecutions. Some of them are not Christians at all, but some are and will be saved "but only as one escaping through the flames." (I Corinthians 3:15) The apostle Paul spoke of some of these people in I and II Timothy. He mentioned Hymenaeus and Alexander. In II Timothy 2:17, he mentioned Hymenaeus again, and Philetus. In II Timothy 4:10, he mentioned Hymenaeus and Philetus again. In II Timothy 4:10, he mentioned Demas. These people could be nonbelievers, but they could also be carnal Christians who might be saved. I remember in seminary when we had a discussion on this particular doctrine: "The eternal security of the believer." Some students said that no body is eternally secure until you die in God's service.

After getting different opinions from the students, the professor who was Dr.Mario Valcin said, and I quote: "If what some of you guys believe was the truth, if there was no eternal security really as some of you believe, it would be better for a person to settle with Satan than with God. Because if after God has saved you, Satan can snatch you out of the hand of God, then Satan is more powerful than God, and therefore better deserves our allegiance."

One of my opponents to that doctrine said: "This doctrine is a demonic doctrine" and he discouraged people from believing in such a teaching.

Jesus himself taught on many occasions this doctrine. In John 10:28, 29, He said: *"I give them (my sheep) eternal life, and they shall never perish; no one can snatch them out of my hand. My Father, who has given them to me is greater than all; no one can snatch them out of my Father's hand."*

6. Why do people believe that their Salvation is not secure?

I am going to suggest some reasons.

(1) They believe in works. But, they forget that the Bible says in Ephesians 2:9, *"Not by works so that no one can boast."*

Some people believe in helping God with their salvation. So they reject the idea that they cannot make a contribution to their salvation. My friend, let me reassure you that you cannot.

(2) They believe in tradition more than they believe in the word of God. The Pharisees and the teachers of the law made the same mistake and

were left behind while the prostitutes and the tax collectors were saved during the ministry of Jesus.

My friend, if you do not stop believing in tradition, the same will happen to you.

(3) They believe in dedication, confirmation and baptism as a way of salvation. Confirmation cannot save you. Baptism cannot save you either. The washing of baptism is symbolic of the blood of Jesus Christ, which really washes your sins and my sins. Water baptism implies three things: a) You make it known publicly that you have confessed Jesus Christ as Lord and Savior. b) Going under water means that you die with Jesus Christ and leave your old self under the water. c) When you come up from under the water, you are confessing symbolically that "I am resurrected with Christ and the new I is no longer in control, but Jesus Christ is." You promise to be a slave of Jesus Christ in every aspect of your life.

All these ceremonies are meaningful only if you really put your faith in the Lord. If not, all you are doing is taking a shower without soap. This is to let you know that water baptism cannot wash away your sins. Only the blood of Jesus Christ can.

Are you washed by the blood of the Lamb of God?

(4) They believe in the Sabbath day to save them. Beloved, unfortunately, the Sabbath is only the rest of the Lord. God also commanded us to labor six days and to rest one day. That was not given as a way of Salvation. The rest is important, but cannot save.

My friend, neither the Sabbath day, nor any of the Ten Commandments can save any person.

So the reason that a lot of people are not assured of their eternal salvation is the fact that they fail to practice the things discussed above, as they should. As a result, they think that they are not eternally secure. But let me ask you a question: When are you going to do that thing you believe is going to make you perfect so that you can be sure of your salvation?

Let us reason together... you have been trying for so long and you keep on failing. When do you think that you are not going to fail anymore?

Do you know that this will never happen? In order for you and me to stop failing, we have to become perfect, and we will never be perfect on earth. There were only three perfect persons who ever lived on the earth. Adam and Eve were perfect before the intervention of sin, and Jesus Christ lived a perfect life while on earth, and that is it. No one else is perfect and no one else will ever be perfect

In other words, what you are looking for in order to become eternally secure is not possible.

The eternal security of the believer is not a result of any work or any accomplishment on his part. On the contrary, it is the result of who gives us the salvation. God is the one who gives it to us, and He is the one who secures it as well. So if you have true saving faith in Jesus Christ, you are saved and secure forever and ever amen! Larry McGill said: "It is the rightful heritage of every believer, even the newest in the family of faith, to be absolutely certain that eternal life is his present possession. To look to self is to tremble. To look to Calvary's finished work is to Triumph."[4]

Let me add this for you to think about. Salvation is a free gift from God. The death and resurrection of Jesus Christ guarantees it. Jesus Christ is the sole reason and the only means of salvation. Every person who puts his trust in Jesus Christ is eternally secure. If there were another way for people to be saved, God would not have sent Jesus Christ to die on the cross.

Jesus said: *"I am the way, and the truth, and the life; no one comes to the Father except through me."* John 14:6.

So my friend, stop believing in works, tradition, sacraments, and commandments for salvation and/or assurance of salvation. Jesus Christ took care of all of these at the cross.

So remember these things – if you trust Jesus Christ with all your heart, you are saved and secure for eternity.

-You cannot be lost after you were saved by the blood of Jesus Christ.

- Don't listen to what any people say about eternal security, but listen to what the Scripture says.

- You need to know now that you are saved and have eternal life, not just after you die. If you want to receive the free gift of God, which is Salvation; pray in this way: "Dear God, I know that I am a sinner. I know that Jesus Christ died for my sins. I am sorry for my sins and I ask Jesus to forgive my sins. Come into my life and save me. Make me secure for eternal life. In Jesus' name I pray. Amen!"

May God grant you the wisdom to listen to the truth and do the right thing before it is too late. I hope to see you in heaven. May God bless you!

Are You A Born-Again Christian Or A So-Called One?

CHAPTER EIGHT

THE CHURCH

1. What is the Church?

The Greek word for church is "ekklésiā" (ek=out, and kletōs =called). The Church is formed of people called out of the world. The church is the business of Jesus Christ. In Matthew 16:18, the Bible says: *"Upon this rock I will build my Church; and the powers of hell shall not prevail against it."* Jesus Christ is the founder and owner of the church. Michael C. Griffiths said: "God thought the Church. Jesus Christ gave Himself for the church. The Holy Spirit built the church in incorporating us in it."[1]

Jesus called people out of the world and formed the church on the day of Pentecost. Acts 2:37-47. Even today, Jesus Christ is still calling people to come to His church. The church was born fifty days after Jesus' resurrection.

After Jesus Christ rose from the dead, he stayed for forty days on earth, ministering to his disciples and others. He told His disciples not to leave Jerusalem until they received what He promised to them, the Holy Spirit. Jesus then went back to heaven and ten days later, He sent the comforter He was talking about, the Holy Spirit who gave birth to the church in Jerusalem.

2. How many Churches are there?

There is only **One** True Church. It is called the Church of Jesus Christ. Remember what Jesus said in Matthew16:18, *"I will build my Church,"* not my Churches. There are many names for the church. It's called the Spiritual church because every member of that church is connected by the Holy Spirit of God. It's also called the universal church because that church is composed of people all over the world. There are Christians in every continent of the world, and we all belong together to the one church of Jesus Christ.

It's also called the mystical and invisible church. In a sense, the church is mystical, because only God knows for sure those who belong to the church.

And it is also invisible since we cannot see all the true members of this universal church all in one place.

There is however what we call the local church. The first one was in Jerusalem. Acts 2 tells us about that church. The local church is a body of believers gathered together to worship the Lord. There are many names for the local church. Here are a few of the names given to the local church by different people.

(1) The assembly of the Saints.
(2) The assembly of believers.
(3) The house of God.
(4) The body of Christ- which also refers to the universal church.
(5) The flock…etc.

Someone might say, why do we call the church of Jesus Christ, the true church? It's simple. It is the only true church there is. Jesus Christ Himself said in Matthew13:30, in the parable of wheat and weeds, *"Let both grow together until the harvest. At that time I will tell the harvesters: first collect the weeds and tie them in bundles to be burned, then gather the wheat and bring it into my barn."* In Matthew7:21, he said: *"Not all who sound religious are really godly people. They may refer to me as "Lord", but still won't get to heaven. For the decisive question is whether they obey my father in heaven."*

What does that mean? This was a reference to the thousands of local churches that we have today in the world. Many people fill the local churches, but very few of them belong to the true church, which is the church of Jesus Christ.

3. Who really belongs to the True Church?

Only born again Christians belong to the true Church. Not church goers, not Protestants, not Catholics, not religious people, not people who have been confirmed and baptized, not people who have accomplished good works, not those who have followed tradition. None of these groups belong to the church of Jesus Christ.

Only born again, Bible believing Christians are members of the invisible church. Who are these people? I am going to list a hundred characteristics of a born again Christian, a true believer of the word of God.

(1) They believe in the virgin birth of Jesus Christ.

(2) They believe that Jesus Christ is the Messiah.

(3) They believe that Jesus Christ is the Son of God.

(4) They believe that Jesus Christ is God.

(5) They believe in the death and physical resurrection of Jesus Christ.

(6) They believe in the two natures of Jesus Christ-100% man and 100% God.

(7) They believe that Jesus Christ is the only way of salvation.

(8) They believe that the sacrifice of Jesus Christ paid for the penalty of their sin.

(9) They believe in the two ordinances of Jesus Christ, baptism and the Lord Super.

(10)They believe in the imminent return of Jesus Christ.

(11) They believe in the two fold return of Jesus Christ, (1st for the church in the air, 2nd with the Saints for the millennial reign).

(12) They believe in the Triune God (Father, Son, and Holy Spirit).

(13) They believe that the Holy Spirit is God.

(14) They believe that salvation is a free gift from God.

(15) They believe in life after death.

(16) They believe in a literal heaven and hell.

(17) They believe that God will judge the world with justice.

(18) They believe in the omnipotent, omniscient, and omnipresent God.

(19) They believe in the Sovereignty of God.

(20) They believe in the providence of God.

(21) They believe in money as a servant, not as a master.

(22) They believe in Creationism, not in Evolution.

(23) They believe in the sanctity of life.

(24) They believe in missions locally, nationally, and globally.

(25)   They love God with all their heart, all their soul, all their mind, and all their strength.

(26)   They submit themselves to the authority of the Scripture.

(27)   They live to please God instead of themselves.

(28)   They humble themselves and lift up the name of Jesus.

(29)   They are committed in their service for God.

(30)   They honor God with their "Time, Talent, and Treasure."

(31)   They listen to, practice, and apply the word of God in their lives.

(32)   They prefer Jesus to their husband or wife, mother or father, brother or sister, son or daughter.

(33)   They are in submission when the Bible speaks.

(34)   They respect the overseer of their soul.

(35)   They pray to God for what they need, and their need is met.

(36)   They are liberal in love, in service, and in giving.

(37)   They have joy in their hearts no matter what.

(38)   They do not forsake their assembly (the local church).

(39)   Their only disobedience is ignorance.

(40)   They are not perfect, but they are forgiven.

(41)   They go to a doctrinally sound local church.

(42)   They participate in the Lord 's Supper regularly.

(43)   They prefer to suffer than to compromise.

(44)   They will persevere in serving Christ no matter what.

(45)   They know that they are eternally secure.

(46) They go to church primarily to worship God.

(47) They do not envy another's position nor are they jealous of another's success.

(48) They worship God with their mouths and their hearts.

(49) They give God the priority in their lives.

(50) They do not do what they want to do, but what God wants them to do.

(51) They consult God in everything that they are doing.

(52) They surrender their will to the Lordship of Jesus Christ.

(53) They read the Scripture regularly and search for the truth.

(54) They do to others as they would like others do to them.

(55) They know that they are saved by Grace, through faith.

(56) They care for the poor, widows, orphans, and strangers.

(57) They visit and pray with the sick and prisoners.

(58) They go to church regularly, except when there is an emergency.

(59) They participate in discipleship and spreading the great commission of Jesus Christ.33.

(60) They support the church with their tithes, and offerings and gifts.

(61) They distinguish right from wrong, and practice the right and refuse to do wrong.

(62) They say yes, and mean it, and no, and mean it.

(63) The Holy Spirit dwells in them.

(64) They do not require an eye for an eye, a tooth for a tooth.

(65) They love others as themselves.

(66) They are always ready to forgive others.

(67) They accept and follow the teachings of the Bible faithfully and obediently.

(68) They are loyal to all the commandments of Jesus Christ.

(69) They call the truth, truth, and a lie, a lie

(70) They do not take sides in a court of law, but only support justice.

(71) They recognize that there is absolute truth.

(72) They are pro-life and anti abortion and opposed to murder of any kind.

(73) They are pro-morality and they strive to live a holy life.

(74) They recognize marriage as the legitimate union of one man and one woman, husband and wife.

(75) They are married for life, except in rare cases of infidelity and/or abandonment.

(76) They are against so-called same sex marriages.

(77) They are for the preservation of society, not for the destruction of it.

(78) They are pro-God and anti-Satan.

(79) They respect and obey the state's authority, as long as its law is not in opposition to the law of God.

(80) They are not afraid to die for what they believe.

(81) "They sometimes lose a battle, but never a war."

(82) They may fail, but they will come back from their failure.

(83) They accept suffering, if it is the will of God for them.

(84) They pray for those who persecute them.

(85) They love their enemies.

(86) They distinguish between the innocent and the guilty.

(87)   They are recognized by their fruits.

(88)   Their actions match their words.

(89)   They apologize when they are wrong.

(90)   They dress properly and decently at all time.

(91)   They might fall into sin, but they do not live in sin.

(92)   They accept themselves as God designed them.

(93)   They learn to wait upon the Lord.

(94)   They respect and obey their parents.

(95)   They do not mistreat their spouse.

(96)   They do not mistreat strangers.

(97)   They sacrifice for others.

(98)   They repay their debt.

(99)   They flee from sin.

(100) They pick up their cross daily and follow the Lord.

Remark: Not all Christians are going to automatically accomplish all these things; however, that will be their goal. They may not have the power to live this way, but they do have the desire to do so, and the more they try to live according to the word of God the better they will do it. Jesus Christ lived like that, so we Christians must strive to do the same.

4. Who should be accepted as a local Church member?

In order to be accepted as a member of the local church, a person should:

(1) Make a profession of faith.

(2) Be baptized as a public testimony of his/her belief in the Lord Jesus Christ.

(3) Be available to participate in all church activities.

(4) Be submissive to all the commands of Jesus Christ.

(5) Agree to be under the watch-care of other believers.

The Bible says in Hebrews 10:24: "And let us consider how we may spur one another on toward love and good deeds."

When you become a born again Christian, you now belong to a new family, the family of God. There will be a lot of new things to learn, some rules to apply, and some guidelines to follow. Paul said in II Corinthians 5: 17: *"Therefore, if anyone is in Christ, he is a new creation; the old has gone, the new has come!"*

You are now ready to receive commands from Jesus Christ himself through the leadership of the church in which you become a member.

Though many people fail to recognize it, it remains a fact that Jesus gives us commands in the Bible, and does not make these things optional. One of the signs that will indicate that you are a true believer is how you receive the commands of Jesus Christ.

In John 14:15, He said: *"If you love me, you will obey what I command."* In verse 21, he said: *"Whoever has my commands and obeys them, he is the one who loves me."*

In John 15:14, he said: *"You are my friends, if you do what I command."*

I believe that if you really desire to be a Christian in your heart, this is not going to be a burden for you; on the contrary, you will rejoice in

137

your newfound family and live life as a friend of our Lord and Savior Jesus Christ.

5. What is the Mission of the Church?

Jesus Christ explained to the disciples the mission of the church even before the institution itself was founded. He wants the church to:

(1) Make disciples. --In Mathew 28:18-20, Jesus said: *"All authority in heaven and on earth has been given to me. Therefore go and make disciples of all nations, baptizing them in the name of the Father and of the Son and of the Holy Spirit, and teaching them to obey everything I have commanded you. And surely I am with you always, to the very end of the age."*

The job of every believer is to make disciples. Are you making disciples? Have you ever told somebody about your encounter with the Lord Jesus Christ and how your life has been changed? If not, you need to start now.

(2) Be a witness. --In Acts 1:8, he told his disciples: *"But you will receive power when the Holy Spirit comes on you; and you will be my witnesses in Jerusalem, and in all Judea and Samaria, and to the ends of the earth."* In Jerusalem (where you are now), in all Judea (your surrounding province), in Samaria (your neighboring countries) and unto the uttermost part of the earth (the world). Are you a witness? If so, what kind of witness are you? Can people see Jesus Christ in your witnessing?

138

(3) Be the salt of the world. In Matthew 5:13a, Jesus said: *"You are the salt of the earth..." Do you understand the meaning of "salt of the earth?"*

   a) Salt gives tastes. When non-believers look at us Christians, do they have an appetite for Jesus Christ or do they feel like their mouths are full of gravel?

   b) Salt makes people thirst. As salt, do we make people want to drink from the water of life, who is Jesus Christ, or do we make them feel "nauseous" instead?

   c) Salt also preserves. In third world countries, even now in the 21st century, they are still using salt to preserve their meat because they do not have refrigerators in many places around the world. As Christians, that is exactly what we should be doing, preserving the world from decaying. Are we doing that, or are we partly responsible for the process of decay?

     I am sure that some of us are doing a good job in preserving the world. However, some of us **are not**. I encourage you to start being part of the solution in preserving the world, and not part of the problem in helping the world go deeper into decay.

     One thing is going to be crystal clear though. When Jesus Christ returns for His church and removes the born again Christians (the salt) from the earth, then the stench of the world will indicate that the salt has been taken away.

(4) Be the light of the world. In Matthew 5:14a, Jesus said: *"You are the light of the world..."* What does the light do?

   a) The light shines.

b)   The light reveals.

c)   The light chases away darkness.

Jesus said: "...People who do bad things don't like the light, because their works are evil, and the light reveals what they are doing..." As a Christian, do you like the light or are you afraid of it? Are you yourself a light for those who are in darkness? Is your light lit for your household, your neighbors, your co-workers, your friends, etc?

(5) Preach the Gospel. Jesus said to his disciples in Mark 16:15: *"go ye into all the world, and preach the gospel to every creature."* Every believer has the responsibility to preach the gospel by different means. You may not have to do it like a preacher in a pulpit, or an evangelist in the stadium but you can preach it by your conduct, by the way you communicate to others.

(6) Warn the world about the danger of sin. It is our duty to let the world know about the poison of sin, and that the blood of Jesus Christ is the only antibiotic for this deadly disease. In Romans 3:23, the Bible says: *"for all have sinned and come short of the glory of God."* In Romans 5:8, we read: *"But God demonstrates His own love for us in this, while we were still sinners, Christ died for us."*

Do you see yourself in this picture, accomplishing the mission of the church? This is my job and your job also, and we must do it!

140

6. When will the *Church age end* on earth?

The church age will end on earth at the sound of the Trump of God. In I Thessalonians 4:16, 17, we read: *"For the Lord himself will come down from heaven, with a loud command, with the voice of an archangel and with the trumpet call of God, and the dead in Christ will rise first. After that, we who are still alive and are left will be caught up with them in the clouds to meet the Lord in the air. And so we will be with the Lord forever."*

Also, at Jesus' ascension, two angels came to speak with the apostles, saying: *"men of Galilee, why do you stand here looking into the sky? This same Jesus, who has been taken from you into heaven, will come back in the same way you have seen him go into heaven."* (Acts 1:11) This can happen at any time, even while you are reading this book. Are you ready? If the trumpet sounds today, will you be heading to heaven with Jesus Christ?

If you are not sure, I encourage you to make sure right now. Just say: "Thank you Jesus for dying for my sins. I recognize that I am a sinner. I repent of my sins. I invite you to come to my life. Change my heart. I want to be like you. I want to live with you in heaven. And I want to go with you when the trumpet sounds. In Jesus' name I pray. Amen!"

7. The Responsibility of the Church Member.

When you become a church member, you need to embrace all the responsibilities that come with it. When you become a member of any club, you do everything that is required of you, don't you?

When you register in any college or university to become a student, you must follow all the disciplinary code, do all your homework, and do everything that is required of you, isn't that true? If not, you are not a real student; very soon you will be let go.

The same is true for someone who joins the armed forces. The person must be submissive and willing to receive training in order to be ready for battle. So beloved, when we become Christians, we must do our share in everything that is required of us as well.

> (1) We must come to church meetings regularly. We should not miss our church services unless there is an emergency.
>
> (2) We must give our time to assist in what we can do in the physical work of the church when that is necessary
>
> (3) If we are to grow in maturity, we must come to all prayer meetings, Bible studies and Sunday school services. The same way that we need food for our body, even so we need the word of God and prayer for our soul and our spirit. Every time that we feed the body once, we should feed the soul and the spirit twice.

(4) We must share our gifts and talents with the church in whatever way may be beneficial to the congregation. Every believer receives one or more gifts from God to praise Him with, and to edify the saints.

(5) We must pay our tithes and offerings, and give gifts, especially when God blesses us in some special way.

(6) We must participate in members' meeting and give our opinions or suggestions that will help build the body of believers even stronger.

(7) We must pray for one another, and pray especially for the leaders of the church. The Pastor(s), the Pastor's wife and family. They are usually the first target of the evil one. Pray also for the unity of the church's members, locally and universally.

(8) We must visit and encourage the sick, and those who are in trouble of any kind. This is not the work of the pastors/leaders only. It is for all believers.

(9) We must avoid all forms of unfounded criticism. Someone has said: "It is easy to criticize, but the art of doing is difficult." Many pastors and/or church leaders have abandoned the church because of those unfounded criticisms.

(10) Finally, watch out for one another and, with a meek spirit, help the brother or sister who

may fall into sin. In Matthew 18:15-17, Jesus said: *"If your brother sins against you go and show him his fault, just between the two of you. If he listens to you, you have won your brother over. But if he will not listen, take one or two others along, so that every matter may be established by the testimony of two or three witnesses. If he refuses to listen to them, tell it to the church; and if he refuses to listen even to the church; treat him as you would a pagan or a tax collector."*

-Warning to all Churchgoers.

We must avoid the **microwave worship** style developed in the United States of America. That means the programmed 55 minutes worship of a lot of American Christians. From 11 o'clock AM to 11:55 AM many so-called Christians fill every church sanctuary in U.S., and they think that they have worshipped God, the God of the universe, their maker. Some of them come to church late and leave early. Some give God 30 minutes a week. Some give 45. Others give an hour and 50 minutes a year (fifty five minutes at Christmas and the other 55 at Easter). Sometimes, I think that God looks at some of us and calls Jesus Christ to come to see a bunch of hypocrites entering hundreds of sanctuaries around the world.

Let us reason together for a moment...there are 10,080 minutes in a week. 10% of 10,080 are 1,008. You give 55 minutes a week to God and you have the gall to say that you are a Christian...! May I ask you two questions? What kind of Christian? And, do you have a receipt to prove that?

Stay 55 minutes a week with your husband/wife in the home and spend all the rest of your time in the street, at work, at school and so on, and then tell your mate "I love you so much!" And see what the response will be. Then compare that to what God might say...! Do you want a role model on giving quality time to God? I have an elder by the name of Paul Duval who gives an average of 15 hours a week in God's service in the church, not counting the hours he gives doing God's work outside the church. If you go to church every week and spend 55 minutes without missing one Sunday, you give 47.6 hours to God in one year. Brother Duval gives approximately **780 hours** a year in God's service in the church alone. Can you imagine the reward of that service both on earth and in heaven? Does that tell you something? Evaluate how you use your time by making your priority list below. Match the numbers with the activities, applying number **1** to the most important activity, and so on.

Here is the priority list:

My sport	1)_____
My family	2)_____
My work	3)_____
My school	4)_____
My God	5)_____
My entertainment	6)_____
My church	7)_____

I hope and pray that you belong to the church of Jesus Christ. If so, press on. Keep the faith. If not, I challenge you to become a true member of the Church right now to guarantee that you will have a joyous eternity with our Lord and Savior Jesus Christ.

8. The Leadership in the Church.

Humanly speaking, the leadership of the church was entrusted to the disciples of Jesus Christ (the twelve, minus Judas, plus Mathias). The half brother of Jesus, James, was also one of the leaders of the church. Paul the apostle was added to this group after his dramatic conversion on the Damascus road.

Many more people became church leaders: the Deacons/Elders, the church fathers, the reformers and so on, until today God is still choosing leaders for His church and will continue to do so until Jesus Christ comes to rapture the Church.

However, not every person who is a leader in the church today is called by God. And that is the reason why we see that so many churches operating more like a business with its clients, or like a club with its customers than like a biblically based church. I think today's generation has more so-called church leaders heading straight to hell than any generation of the past. You might say, why? Well, I am about to tell you some of the reasons for such a statement.

(1) They are more interested in the material side of the church than the spiritual.

(2) They are insensitive about sins in the church. They use a sheet to cover up sins by saying: "Everybody sins." In saying this, they shut

the mouth of any person who might want to say something about the sins that are destroying the church today.

(3) They let their church members do as they wish, as long as they bring in their tithes and offerings.

(4) They are mercenaries, not shepherds.

(5) They are professional preachers, not preachers with a true calling from God.

(6) They are grabbers of dollars, not fishers of men.

(7) They believe more in marketing strategies for the growth of the church, than in prayers, evangelization and sanctification.

I was looking for a place for our church to meet and worship. When I found one, the pastor of the church asked for my schedule. When I presented one to him, he looked at it and saw our prayer schedule, and he said: "I hope that your prayer schedule is not contagious!" I said I wished it was for all Christian churches in the whole world.

Now, who should be church leaders for today and tomorrow?

In the Old Testament, God chose the leaders of the Temple. The priests and the Levites began with Aaron and the tribe of Levi. Numbers 3:5-12

He chose Samuel Himself. (I Samuel 3:1-14). He chose all the good prophets from Abraham to John the Baptist and all the New Testament prophets (Acts 13:1).

In the New Testament Jesus chose the disciples (Luke 6:12-16)

He chose Paul (Acts 9:1-16). Later on he chose the church fathers, then the reformers, and so on until today.

First: The church leader must be called by God himself. Many people are called to be saved by God, but not to be ministers, preachers or pastors, and evangelists. People need a special call from God for these positions.

Second: The church leader must be a converted, sanctified, loyal, faithful, obedient servant of Jesus Christ.

Third: The church leader must be a daily student of the word of God, and a person of prayer.

Fourth: The church leader must be a moral and spiritual person.

Fifth: The church leader must have good credit in the opinion of Christians and non-Christians alike.

Sixth: The church leader must set a good example for others to follow, beginning with his own household, and he must be beyond reproach.

Seventh: The church leader must be able to lead the flock, instead of getting them lost.

Any good leader must be able to see a few miles ahead of the people he is leading.

I encourage you, if you are a church leader, to ask yourself these questions: "Am I called by God to lead his church..." "Why am I in ministry?" "Am I pleasing God or man in my ministry?"

Are women called to lead the church as pastor? We may see many women pastors today in the church; however, with all humility, I say that it is not God's plan for a woman to be pastor.

From the Old Testament to the New Testament, God never chose a woman to lead his people.

In the Garden of Eden, Adam was in charge of his household. That is why God called Adam to account even when Eve was the one who first sinned. God chose Moses and Aaron to lead his people from Egypt to the Promised Land.

The priests, the Levites were all men who served in the Temple

When Jesus Christ chose the twelve apostles, he did not choose one woman. There was no woman writer of the Old or New Testament (not even Ruth and Esther). They are not the writers of the books that bear their names

There was no woman among the first leaders of the church. When we read the qualifications for the church pastorate, we find no feminine descriptions for the pastoral candidate. Look at I Timothy 3:1-7 "…If any one set his heart on being an overseer, **he** desires a noble task… The husband of one wife (not wife of one husband)… **his** children must obey **him (not her** children)… If anyone does not know how to manage **his** own family, how can **he** take care of God's church?... **He** must not be a recent convert **(not she)… He** must also have a good reputation **(not she),** etc.

The same is repeated in Titus 1:5-9. The Bible prohibits the woman from taking authority over man. In I Timothy 2:11, 12 we read: *"A woman should learn in quietness and full submission. I do not permit a woman to teach or to have authority over a man; she must be silent."* Some more instructions were given in verses 13-15, *"For Adam was formed first, then Eve. And Adam was not the one deceived; it was the woman who was deceived and became a sinner. But woman will be saved through childbearing- if they continue in faith, love and holiness with propriety."* Also in I Corinthians 14:34, 35, *"Women should remain silent in the churches. They are not allowed to speak, but must be in submission, as the Law says. If they want to inquire about something, they should ask their own husbands at home; for it is disgraceful for a woman to speak in the church."*

Though there were a few women who received a short mission in the Bible, it was not a charge to lead the church (Huldah, II Kings 22:14-20; Deborah, Judges 4:4; Miriam who took the lead in praising the Lord in a hymn for a short time, Exodus 15:20).

In the New Testament there were women like Phoebe who only carried a letter to the Romans; she probably was a deaconess (Romans 16:1). Mary Magdalene carried a message to the disciples of Jesus after his resurrection, but that was not a call to ministry. That was a message, not the great commission.

If you are a woman and you feel like you have a call to ministry, maybe you have a call to become a pastor's wife, so you can work close with your husband as pastor. You might still want to go to seminary to prepare yourself to help your husband in the administration of the church, but not to be pastor of a local church, because it is against God's will.

As a Christian woman, whom would you want to please, God or yourself? I believe that nothing is better for a Christian than to live a life that is pleasing to God. The most important call of God to a Christian woman is to be a wife and a mother to take care of her household. It doesn't mean that she cannot work outside the home, but if she does her household must be set in order first (Proverbs 31:10-31). I mentioned earlier that my mom started working at a very early age, but guess what? When she was married she quit her job to raise her family. After the family was raised, she went back to work for the same missionary couple. At that time, my older brother and I were already in high school. The fact is that she put the priority on what was most important for that time; she raised five great children who are now bringing thousands into the kingdom of God. She did not focus her attention on money, but sought to please God by doing what the word of God said. And in so doing, she is now building the kingdom of God from generation to generation. Christian women, if you seek to please God and his word, you will do much more to further his work than if you do something which you want to do in the church, which, nevertheless, is against the word of God. Remember, "Obedience is worth more than sacrifice."

9. The Christian Dress Code.

Our generation has the worst record in the way we dress in the history of the church. Modern-day so-called Christians show more disrespect to God in the way they dress than any other generation from the first century until today.

Our mouths talk much about God, but our hearts are as far from God as the East is from the West. We dress up to go to church the same way we dress up to go to a nightclub. At the same time we call ourselves Christians. We prevent people from coming to God by our depraved behavior.

I believe that this began in the 1920's in the U.S.A. and then spread to the western world like wildfire. You can read that for yourself in American History where it is said: "In the 1920's, a woman would have shocked people if she came to a party wearing a skirt that was just long enough to cover her knees. Women had always worn long skirts that covered their ankles. Women dared to wear shorter skirts because America changed during the 1920's."[2]

"The 1920's were called the Roaring Twenties. It was a time when American culture changed in many ways. New fashions, music, literature, and entertainment appeared in the 1920's. Fashions changed when women said good-bye to long skirts. Instead they wore short skirts, pants, and shorts. They also wore short hair cuts and used make up."[3]

Robert Turner, Jr. said: "Some said that World War I was the end of American innocence. Perhaps it was. America was a different place in the 1920's right after the war. Racial strife broke out anew. The struggle for women's rights began again. Women fashions became bold and daring. Many women began to cut their hair short. Many more shocked people by wearing dresses above their knees. A new way of dancing also shocked people, and there were new and different kinds of poems, novels, and music,"[4]

I don't know how many of us have noticed that in less than a century from that behavioral change, the church has become one with the world. Ladies in many so-called churches dressed up in the same way that prostitutes do, even worst in some cases. Some come to church practically naked. If they drop a pen on the floor, they cannot pick it up, since people will see their undergarments. Some ladies go to church with the specific goal of seducing one or more men. Pants became the way of dressing up for many women. Nobody says anything. No leadership, no watchdog group-or conservative Christian organization takes a stand to prevent this kind of lawlessness in the Church.

Do you know that pants were designed for men, not for women? Pants will never fit a Christian woman without causing dire damage to women, to the family, to the church and to society. This will cause, certainly, family break ups, church degradations, rapes, and more problems for the authorities. God said in Deuteronomy 22:5, *"A woman must not wear men's clothing, nor a man wear women's clothing, for the Lord your God detests anyone who does this."*

Have you ever noticed how they identify man and woman on a bathroom door? Have you ever noticed a woman with pants on, on the door? Have you ever thought about that? If pants fit women so well, why not have a woman with pants on a bathroom door.

Aren't we, as Christians, supposed to be leaders in every good thing, including morality? Then how come we become like monkeys who just watch what others do and copy them? How come the world for us Christians becomes like water in a receptacle? When you put water in a cup, it takes the shape of the cup. When you put it in a pot, it takes the shape of the pot. If you put it on a plate, it becomes flat just as the plate. We are just like that with the world unfortunately! When we should be leaders in all good things, we become followers in bad things. Instead of the world copying us, we copy the world. We become like a bunch of puppies that are being manipulated by dry bones, thinking that they have marrow inside them.

I believe that it is time to wake up. We need to go back in history and find out what it means to be Christians. Write to the Billy Graham Evangelistic Association and order a video copy of his crusades in the seventies, even the eighties, and see how Christian women used to dress, and do the same if you don't want to be fried in the fire of hell.

Remember that the way you dress reveals whether you are a born again Christian or a so-called one. According to the Bible, a woman, not a girl, needs to wear a veil and can not cut her hair short in the church of God. For this is against the will of God. Men, on the other hand, need to cut their hair short and cannot wear a hat in the church of God. There is no "Rasta" Christian. When you are converted to Christianity you have to change your life style also.

It is against the word of God for Christians to have tattoos. In Leviticus 19:28 we read: *"Do not cut your bodies for the dead or put tattoo marks on yourselves. I am the Lord."*

I once invited a fellow worker to church. He gave me a fake smile and paused for a moment. I asked him why he was acting as he did. He told me that he grew up in the church; however, when he became a teenager, he left the church and went his own way. He continued to tell me that his mother is always praying for him, and he wants to go back to church from time to time. However, every time he tries, he is so disappointed that he stopped altogether. He said the last two times he went to church, he could not figure out where he was. He had to keep reminding himself that he was in church, because he felt like he was in a nightclub. Most of the women in the church dressed up just like strippers and they acted like they were offering praises to the Lord. "This," he said, "I call hypocrisy of the worst kind."

Who are responsible for such a mess in the local church? They are many.

The first group of people responsible for this situation is the **leaders** of the church. They are unable to lead. Many church leaders today follow the leadership style of Aaron and reject the leadership model of Moses. Aaron said, "Whatever you want, I want also." Moses, on the other hand, stood firm on the word of God. Do you remember the consequences of the sin of Aaron and Israel? Read it for yourself in Exodus 32:1-35. As Christians, why don't we follow the example of men like Mordecai who would not bow down to worship anybody but God? Or like Esther who was queen, but put her life in jeopardy to fight for the people of God? (Esther 3:3-6; 4:14) Or men like Daniel, Shadrac, Meshac and Abed Nego who stood firm even when facing the furnace of fire heated seven times hotter and the lion's den? (Daniel 3:8-18; 6:16-24) Consider Stephen in the New Testament who stood firm for the truth even when they stoned him to death (Acts 7:1-60). What could we say about the apostles Peter and Paul facing crucifixion? History reports that when they were about to crucify Peter, his only request was to crucify him up side down, because he was not worthy to be crucified like Jesus Christ.

And concerning Paul, history reports that Nero told Paul, "I am going to kill you by removing your head from your body!" And Paul replied: "Your Majesty, you can not kill a dead man!"

A second group ruining the testimony of the Church is the so-called **Christian artists.** They bring the world with them into the church, and the church leaders sit down and watch the teenagers go crazy for these people and say nothing for the fear of losing the teens, their parents and the fans. So, before you know it, the church becomes the world inside a four-walled religious building. The sermons change and the worship is very different. The Bible is no longer the focus of the church.

Prayer meetings are avoided. And the church becomes like fraternal organization or social club].

I agree that there are some great Christian artists in the church for whom we thank God. However, I speak about those who come to destroy the church by their ridiculous life style.

The church of Jesus Christ deserves some respect. Jesus died for the church. That means a lot for true believers. I know many good Christian artists who do a great job in their singing ministry. I pray and encourage them to keep it up. But for the others, I warn you to change your life style, if you want to go to heaven.

If you need a model woman artist who dresses appropriately, I recommend, among many others, Sister Hermana L.Emile. Invite her to come to sing in your church, and you will not be disappointed in regards to either her songs or style of dress. For you who are Christian artists, both male and female, you need to ask yourself these questions from time to time: (1) Do I sing to please God or to satisfy myself? (2) Do I sing to edify the saints or am I so interested in selling CD's that I am also selling sex? If you want to do the latter, then the church is not the right place for such a business.

I think that a dress code should be imposed for all Christian gatherings. That includes the church, the Christian Television network, the Christian wedding ceremony, the Christian funeral and every gathering where Christians are the organizers.

I visited a Christian church a few years ago with two of our parents who came to visit this country. It was a very sad experience for me, and worst for them. We saw so many naked women walking in the church that we had to leave before the service ended. I am sick of hearing people say: "God does not pay attention to people's clothing; he only looks at the heart." This is "rubbish." People who repeat this trash need to go back to the Bible and they will discover that God gave a dress code even to the priests, men who were supposed to enter his presence (Exodus 28:1-43).

It is said in the Bible that we need to dress decently to come into the presence of God. I Timothy 2:9: *"I also want women to dress modestly, with decency and propriety, not with braided hair or gold or pearls or expensive clothes." Titus 2:3: "Likewise, teach the older women to be reverent in the way they live, not to be slanderers or addicted to much wine, but to teach what is good."*

How many of you think that God will accept your worship if when you go to church you have already insulted him by the way you are dressed? If you were invited to meet with President George W. Bush of the United States or Queen Elizabeth of England, how would you dress? Would you wear your blue jeans, your shirt on top of your pants and sneakers on your feet? With tattoos on your arms, your hair one side up, the other down, two different earrings, a gold tooth, and you are going to meet the president, or the queen? Or would you dress differently? If you would fix yourself up to meet a human dignitary, how much more important it is to dress properly, with your best suit and tie, with a clean shave and a nice hair cut, and wearing the best shoes you own to come into the presence of the almighty God, the one who holds in his power your very breath! You need to think about that, and the next time you hear a preacher excusing such disreputable dress, you will know to walk out of this church, because the preacher is self proclaimed, and not called by God.

There is a third group that is partially responsible for not doing enough, the **conservative Christians** who remain silent. Remember what the Rev. M.L King Jr. said in the struggle for civil rights in Birmingham, Alabama: "The ultimate tragedy of Birmingham is not the brutality of the bad people, but the silence of the good ones."

We need some Christian watchdogs in every good local church. There is no church without discipline. If there is no discipline in a church, it's stopped being a church. It's become a club, a fraternity group or some other kind of gathering, but it is no longer a church. Do you remember what Jesus did when they made the temple a market place in Jerusalem? He was so mad that he started to whip people and turn over the tables with their merchandise. (John 2:13-16)

Here are some examples of Christian clothing:

Yes

No

Yes

Yes

No

Yes

No

Are You A Born-Again Christian Or A So-Called One?

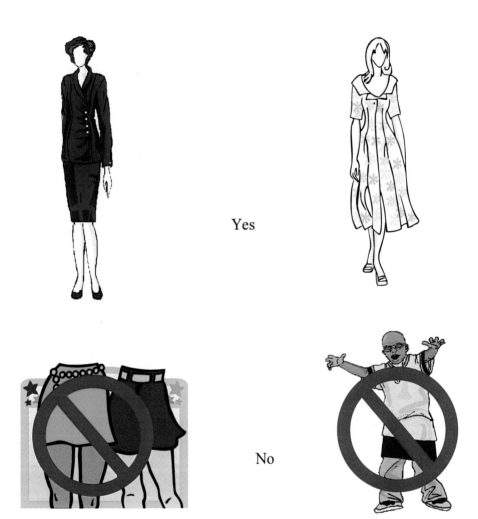

Yes

No

10. Gossips in the Church.

Jesus said: "*If anyone causes one of these little ones who believe in me to sin, it would be better for him to have a large millstone hung around his neck and to be drowned in the depths of the sea.*" (Matthew 18:6) Some people go to church just to gossip about others. They watch every dress somebody wears in order to take note and criticize that sister who can afford to own only two dresses.

There are people in the church who act like they have a lot of compassion for others, and that is their way of knowing what's going on in other people's lives so they can feed their addiction to gossip. Some so-called Christians cannot live without some kind of trouble going on in the church. When there is none for a few weeks, they create one. Beloved, we need to watch our tongue. James said: "Likewise the tongue is a small part of the body, but it makes great boasts. Consider what a great forest is set on fire by a small spark. The tongue also is a fire, a world of evil among the parts of the body. It corrupts the whole person, sets the whole course of his life on fire, and is itself set on fire by hell."

Pastor Stenio Jean Tilus of Miami, Florida said: It is not without reason that God put the tongue inside a barricade of thirty-two posts with chains. The reason is, it's a dangerous piece of weapon." As Christians, how do we use our tongue? Do you use your tongue to build up the church or to destroy it?

Do you use your tongue to praise, pray and give thanks to God or to slander, murder and kill? Remember, you will give an account for every word that comes out of your mouth.

Matthew 12:36 *"But I tell you that men will have to give account on the Day of Judgment for every careless word they have spoken."* Beloved, do not gossip with the pretext that you are making an exhortation in the name of God. Jesus gave clear instructions about helping a falling brother or sister. Matthew18: 15-18.

(1) Try to win over your brother by just you and him/her meeting together. If he/she listens to you, you win them back. But be sure to keep quiet about it. Don't on your way home call ten persons to make a report.

(2) If your brother/sister does not listen to you, you should take one or two others with you as witnesses. If your brother/sister listens to you, you win them back. Again, only you and the ones who went with you need to know about what took place. No one else.

(3) If still your brother or sister will not listen to you, then tell the church. Now everybody can know. But you must take the first two steps before you have recourse to the third one. When you do it the right way, you will have credit in God's eyes, but when you do it in the wrong way, you lose your credit. *"Whatever you do, work at it with all your heart, as working for the Lord, not for men."* Colossians 3:23

11. Pride in the Christian Church.

How proud are you?

In Proverb 16:18 the Bible says: *"Pride goes before destruction, a haughty spirit before a fall."*

Do you know that you cannot be a Christian and be full of pride at the same time? These two don't go together. Do you know that Jesus

Christ, the founder of Christianity, was the most humble person who ever lived on earth? Do you know that many people pretend to be Christians by what they say, but act like Satanists in what they do, all because of pride?

It is certain that every person needs to be proud of himself/herself, but within limits. Only to avoid low self esteem.

Test yourself on how much pride you have. How do you think about yourself compared to others?

I always think that I am better than other people.

I sometimes think that I am better than other people.

I never think that I am better than other people.

I rarely think that I am better than other people.

I used to think that I was better than other people.

Evaluate yourself with this pride thermometer.

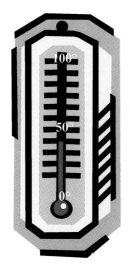

What is your pride level ?

When we look at what Jesus Christ did to come to save us in Philippians 2, I think that His pride limit would be at 50°. To me, that is the limit for a good self-esteem. As for me, I put myself at 50° also. As for you, what is yours?

In conclusion, church leaders, conservative Christians, you need to reinstate sanctions in the local church. We cannot abandon the old discipline of excommunication. Remember, we all will have to give an account, but for those who are leaders more will be required of you. *"Not many of you should presume to be teachers, my brothers, because you know that we who teach will be judged more strictly,"* James 3:1. If you cannot lead, do yourself a favor; take yourself out of the picture.

My beloved, make sure that you represent Jesus Christ the right way, so that you won't have to face the lion of the tribe of Judah in the last day.

CHAPTER NINE

CHRISTIAN LIVING

1. How important is Marriage in a Society?

Because of the foreknowledge of God as to what a society should be, he instituted marriage to be the foundation of Society. In other words, if you take marriage out of the equation of society, you destroy society altogether.

Among the three major institutions that have existed on planet earth (the family, the government and the church), the family, which is the result of marriage, is the oldest and the most important one.

You cannot make a good leader out of someone who was raised without any family structure and upbringing. If society is to continue, then marriage must be honored, respected and preserved.

The Bible says: *"Marriage should be honored by all, and the marriage bed kept pure, for God will judge the adulterer and all the sexually immoral."* Hebrews 13: 4. Marriage is indispensable in a society and must be protected as God instituted it. Man has no right to add to or to take away anything from marriage. God instituted marriage in exactly the right way. All man has to do is to keep and preserve it. Nobody has the right to redefine marriage. It defined by God himself as the union of one man and one woman. The first marriage was the union of a male and a female placed together by God himself, Adam and Eve, husband and wife. When two people are

165

united in marriage, they must be able to reproduce unless there is a medical problem of some kind.

The ceremony of a Christian marriage should be celebrated by a religious figure such as a Rabbi, a Pastor, a Priest or other ordained religious officer. God is more concerned about the religious than the political. He celebrated the first marriage Himself, and before He instituted the government. No born again Christian can be satisfied with a marriage ceremony celebrated in a secular court. The Christian has to go to obtain a marriage license from the court, but he does not have to be married by a clerk of the court who may be living in sin, and not even married himself. The state's involvement in marriage is good; it helps protect against polygamy and guaranties the material possessions of everybody in case of separation and/or divorce.

If you are a Christian couple and you were married by the state, you need to go and receive the blessings of God on your marriage through a religious figure who has received ordination by the church hierarchy.

- Choosing a Partner.

A Christian man was thinking about marriage. He saw a beautiful young woman who pleased him. So, he started dating her. He went and told an older man who was like a mentor to him about the young woman he was dating. Then the older man who believed in God's word asked him: "Did you pray to ask God to choose a woman for you?" The young man replied "No." He said to the young man, "That is what you need to do. Go and pray to ask God if this woman is the right person for you to marry…" So the man left and did what he was told to do. A few days went by and the man came back to his mentor and said: "I've been praying ever since I spoke with you, but nothing has happened!" The mentor told him: "Be patient and wait a few more days, God will surely speak with you!" The young man went home and continued to pray as he was told to do. About three to four days later he came back to his mentor. The mentor asked him: "What is happening?" He said, "I had a dream last night." The mentor said: "Tell me about the dream." He said: "I saw in my dream that I was talking to her and she was standing on a Bible." Then the mentor said: "How do you understand the dream?" He said, "I think that she has no respect for God and the Bible." Then the mentor said: "Do you want to marry someone like that?" "No," he answered. Have you noticed the importance of prayer? I hope so!

The Christian should marry only another Christian with the same faith. That is possible only by prayer to God, the only One who knows the heart of a person. In Jeremiah 17:10, God said: *"I the Lord search the heart and examine the mind..."* And when you do that, you need to put aside all kind of prejudices. If you think that you are so smart and do not need God's assistance in choosing a mate, you might end up marrying a monster.

The signs to look for in a prospective mate:

(1) How fearful is this person of the Lord?
(2) How respectful is this person towards the church, the Bible and the things of God?
(3) How respectful is this person to his/her parents and to government and religious authorities?
(4) How often does this person go to church?

(5) Does the person pay tithes and offerings?

(6) How temperate is this person in everyday affairs?

(7) What is this person's belief about marriage, whether it is for life or until the feeling he/she calls love expires?

For those who quote the famous author who said: "Love is blind!" there is also a not so famous author who said: "Marriage opens the eyes."

It is very important to know a little bit about your prospective mate. Almost everybody is looking for love and affection in a marriage, especially women. A little background about your future husband/wife would help. Remember that you cannot buy love and affection, and they do not grow on a tree, nor can you learn about them in school. You can only pass on what you have received.

That is to say: If you marry somebody who received no love and affection from his/her parents, chances are, you are not going to receive any either…! Marriage is a lasting covenant. In Matthew 19:5, 6, we read: *"for this reason a man will leave his father and mother and be united to his wife, and they will become one flesh. So they are no longer two, but one. Therefore what God has joined together, let man not separate."*

Christian couples should not look at divorce as an alternative. God said in Malachi 2:16: *"I hate divorce."* **Then He signed His name under it:** *"The Lord God of Israel."* Do you know that is the only true God there is? Yes, the God of Abraham, Isaac and Jacob or Israel is the only true and living God.

When you make divorce an option in your marriage you have a 50% chance of getting a divorce. But when you don't make it an option in your marriage, you have a 99% chance of not getting a divorce. The word divorce is evil. Remember what Jesus said to the religious leaders of his time: *"Moses permitted you to divorce your wives because your hearts were hard. But it was not this way from the beginning."* Matthew 19:8.

Divorce is tolerated, not accepted by God only on the ground of marital unfaithfulness and/or abandonment. Matthew 19:9-
I Timothy 5:8

Abandonment is usually the result of unfaithfulness. Protestant churches need to be careful before they remarry divorced people. I think that we need to imitate the Catholic Church in this matter!

- Concerning the so-called homosexual union.

It is nonsense to use such an absurd expression! Nobody in his or her right mind can tolerate such a thing legally in any society. One of the reasons why God created the government is to restrain evil. Homosexuality is evil and must be restrained by the government. Homosexuality is "un-natural" against nature. Though man, as to moral character, is the lowest mammal, in this matter, man should imitate the animals. In the whole universe, has anybody ever noticed an animal coupled with another animal of the same sex? That never has happened and never will happen. Why then should a government allow such an abomination and bring down the curse of God on its people?

Warning—Any country or government that legalizes any form of civil union for homosexual couples needs to be aware of the consequences as well. The God, who destroyed Sodom and Gomorrah for this sin thousands of years ago, is still on the throne, and He will surely bring His judgment on all nations that participate in such an infamy.

But, guess what? Because of the love of God, His patience and compassion you can still come back from your evil ways and he will receive you. You must repent and abandon your sins, and you will receive forgiveness from God. But if you refuse, be prepared for His judgment. Read Amos Chapter 4 and you will see an example of God's judgment.

We Christians do love the people who practice homosexuality, but we hate homosexuality itself. So what we are doing is praying for these people to surrender their life to Jesus in repentance.

2. How important is Moral Value for a Society?

Without good and solid moral values, a society is dying and is subject to destruction sooner or later. Sodom and Gomorrah were destroyed when their moral values sank so low that God's limit of patience was passed. So, the only solution was to eliminate them completely from the face of the earth. You can read the full report in Genesis chapters 18 and 19.

When God promised to give to Abraham the Land of Canaan, there were seven nations who lived there. But they were great sinners, immoral people who lived anyway they saw fit. God gave them enough time to come to their senses, but they kept going down until they reached the point of no return. So, the only option left was destruction. So God destroyed them by the swords of Joshua and the army of Israel. The book of Joshua gives all the details of that destruction.

Abortion- Christians, Beware!

Abortion can be made legal but it will always be immoral. From Genesis to Revelation the Bible says: *"Do not kill or murder."* This is one of the Ten Commandments of God, the creator of the universe. Exodus 20:13, *"You shall not murder."* Abortion is killing innocent people, or rather innocent babies. When you abort a baby (fetus), you kill a person and you become a murderer in the eyes of God. I know that many of you may have done that in ignorance. Now what you need to do is to confess that sin to God and ask for forgiveness, and the merciful God will forgive you. Also you need to pray and advise those who still are committing such a crime by killing their babies and don't even realize what they are doing.

Abortion should not be permitted in a Christian nation like the United States of America. If any of the founding fathers of the U.S were still alive when the highest court of the land voted to make abortion legal, they would have died immediately of a heart attack. To these men, it would have been unconceivable that something like that would ever happen in the United States of America.

However, when you abandon God, when you remove prayer from the public schools and the public square, when you remove the Ten Commandments from court rooms, when you remove the Bible from every public institution, when you elect atheists to public offices, when you approve the homosexual life style, when you give an okay to so called homosexual couples to adopt children, when you prevent teachers from disciplining their students and parents from spanking

171

their children, then you must also know that, when God is voted out in any country, Satan is automatically voted in. Now you also need to get ready for what will happen.

(1) You are going to need more police officers.

(2) You are going to need more weapons.

(3) You are going to need more prisons.

(4) You are going to need more guards for the prisons.

(5) You are going to need more court rooms and judges.

(6) You are going to need more law enforcement officers.

(7) And you are going to need more money or a bigger budget for law and order.

You might say, why would all these consequences take place? Remember the law of cause and effect...

When you reject the Bible, which expounds the highest moral code, you are going to see a lot of every kind of bad thing happening. You are going to have more robbers, more rapists, more corrupt people, more prostitutes, more drug dealers, more alcoholics, and in general, more law breakers. It is important to remember that there will be a consequence for everything that we do. Moral values are some of the most important ingredients in preserving a society. If you despise moral values, you are heading for disaster.

3. What should be the Relationship Between Employer and Employee; Contractor and Customer; *Professional* and Client?

A. Employer and Employee

If you are a Christian employer, the golden rule should be your motto in regard to your employees. *Jesus said in Matthew 7:12: "So in everything, do to others what you would have them do to you..."* Your employees do treat you with respect and dignity. You should also treat your employees with respect and dignity. God will honor that.

Well, do you notice that Jesus Christ modeled the life that he wants us to live and the things that he wants us to do? He walked with His disciples for three and a half years to show them what to say or do and how to say or do it.

My Dad used to say: "You need two goods to make one perfect." I think that this makes sense, don't you? Many conflicts arise between employer and employee for the simple reason that the employer discriminates against or shows prejudice toward the employee or treats the employee like a slave. Do you remember that the reason you give the employee a paycheck is because he/she has worked for you for many hours or days!

It is good that you can provide work for other people... but you need somebody to get the job done, don't you? Usually our attitude is: "I can get somebody else...!" My friend, brother/sister, it is not so easy to maintain such an attitude in the face of God and Jesus Christ...! Jesus said: "I am the defense of the defenseless...I will avenge the weak..." Benefits in the work place are declining very fast in the U.S.

173

and maybe around the world. American employers used to be proud to provide good jobs with good pay and benefits for their fellow American employees; but now it is completely different. American employers are now more concerned about their profits than about their fellow American. Jobs are now shipped overseas where they use child labor, or even Christian slaves in prison for their faith in countries like China, so they can make the maximum profit possible while their fellow Americans are losing the only house they own because they have to accept at least 25% pay cut in order to survive. So, in other words, many Americans now practically become slaves to other fellow Americans. They work with no benefits whatsoever and with a pay check which they have to supplement with a credit card in order to survive; while their employer lives in a mansion, owns a luxury boat, drives a $100,000 automobile and so forth. But, as a Christian employer, how do you look at it? Do you think that it is in your best interests to keep all the profits for yourself and your family and give only a piddling amount to the employees who help make it possible?

Jesus said: *"The worker deserves his wages..."* Luke 10: 7 and this includes all the benefits possible.

I have a brother in Christ by the name of Michelet Emile who has a radio talk show. One day while we were going to the station for a program, I asked him how the week had gone? He said: "Thanks to God, everything was fine. Something good happened for my friend and I am rejoicing with him." Then I asked, "What is it?" Then he explained to me what an employer had done for his faithful employee of about 20 years. That employee was caught up in working two jobs for over 20 years because his plan to go to college had failed. So as a result he was condemned to work two jobs for the rest of his life.

One day, his employer called him up and asked him: "Ever since I've known you, you are always working two jobs; why is that?" He explained the reasons to his boss. Then he told him: "Tomorrow, bring your mortgage statement to me." When he did, his employer took it, paid the mortgage off, and told the man, "I want you to work only one job from now on…!" I praise God for such an employer and I pray that God would touch the heart of thousands of successful employers to imitate his example around the world to bring love, compassion and relief to their employees. Employers, don't fail to give good benefits including raises to your employees when they deserve it. I know one employer who could not give bonuses to his employees in December because it was supposedly a bad year. However this employer took three lavish vacations in the first quarter of the following year. And one of them was in Las Vegas where he took a large sum of money to gamble. When this news leaked out to the employees, they were not too happy about it.

I know most Christian employees are working the best way they know how to please their employer. However, there are some who are not. I want to encourage those of you who are doing well to keep it up. But those who are not, I encourage you to change your ways. Remember that you are Christ's representative in your workplace. Your behavior will either advance the gospel of Christ or push it back.

Remember that your real employer is God Himself. God is the owner of everything and of everybody on the face of the planet. Psalm 24:1 says: *"The earth is the Lord and everything in it, the world, and*

175

all who live in it": If your employer on earth fails to reward you for what you deserve, God, who is your real employer, will not fail to recompense you for what you have done.

In Hebrews 6:10 the Bible says: *"God is not unjust; he will not forget your work..."*

In Revelation 22:12, the Bible says: *"Behold, I am coming soon! My reward is with me, and I will give to everyone according to what he has done."*

Christian employers, what do you think about the Christian Sabbath? I have repeatedly cited the Ten Commandments throughout this book. I believe that will remind us of the word of God. Some employers who are Christians rest on Sunday, but their employees who are also Christians cannot. I think that is wrong! In Exodus 20:8-11 the Bible says: *"Remember the Sabbath day by keeping it holy. Six days you shall labor and do all your work, but the Seventh day is a Sabbath to the Lord your God. On it you shall not do any work, neither you, nor your son or daughter, nor manservant or maidservant, nor your animals, nor the alien within your gates..."*

One of the elders in our church, Bro. Frank Colas, once went to work for a Christian enterprise. He did it on purpose since he is the maestro of the Church's choir and must be at church regularly. However, they put him on schedule to work on Sunday, and when he refused to do so, he was let go. Fellow Christians, what do you think? To me that is wrong in light of what the Bible says. My suggestion is, if you have to have somebody working for you on your Sabbath day, it ought to be a non-Christian. If not, we send the wrong message. Do you recall the story of Paul, Onesimus and Philemon? Onesimus was a slave of Philemon. When he converted to Christianity, his status changed. He was no longer a slave, but a brother. Read it for yourself in Philemon 1:8-17. I encourage you to think more carefully about what you do, so that your actions match your message.

B) Contractor and Customer.

I live in the State of Florida in the U.S.A. I know many people who are victims of bad contractors, especially after a hurricane. I know that a true believer or a Christian is not going to steal money from people and not deliver what he promised his customers, but some so-called Christian will. I became a victim of that with a so-called Christian contractor that we signed a contract with. He did the work. I paid him for his services. A year and a half later, when I went to refinance I found out that there was a lien on my house. The lien was from the same company that I paid fully for the work done. So, you, Christians, beware of wolves in sheep's clothing!

Contractors, do what you have promised to do. Perform the service well in the time frame that you promised unless there are mitigating factors such as problems previously unknown. You are in business to make a profit. Make sure that your profit is fair and can be blessed by the Lord.

The golden rule applies also to contractors and customers.

Customer, keep your word whether given in writing or not. You have agreed to pay a certain amount of money for the work. When the job is done, pay the money. Do not say, "You charged me too much…" and other such things after the job is complete. "Let your yea be yea and your nay be nay." If you don't do what is right and keep your word, you may end up having to face Judge Judy. She will put you in your small shoes, meaning she will humiliate you in front of the world. Plus, if it is Judge Joe Brown, you will end up paying a lot more, when he calculates time and compound interest of about 24.99%.

C) Professional and Client.

Everybody at some time in life will need the help of a professional, maybe a pastor/priest/rabbi, a doctor, an attorney, an accountant, a realtor, a salesperson, an insurance agent, for example. You might need to get married or have a funeral service for a family member. You may be in good health now, but you don't know when you are going to be sick. Sometime you might need the assistance of an attorney for a crime you did not commit; or you might need the help of an accountant for the IRS or for your business. A realtor will be helpful in your real estate dealings and you will need all kinds of insurance. If not today, then tomorrow, you will need some kind of professional assistance one way or another.

We all know that some professionals are Christians who have high moral standards, but many are not what they claim to be.

My call to you who claim to be a Christian is to live up to that profession.

(1) You need to make sure that you have a calling to the profession that you are in.

(2) Make sure that money is not your **god,** that you just see money in dealing with your clients and not the person to whom you are rendering a service.

- If you are a surgeon, do not operate on a patient in order to benefit from the **insurance money**. Value the life of the person **before the profit**. If you are a medical doctor, serve your patients well. My family doctor is Dr. Frage Valcourt; you cannot go to his office and not be satisfied. He takes his time to consult with you and tells you everything in detail and makes sure that you understand. He serves his patients well, he and his staff. I have met people who drive over 200 miles to come to see him. I think that this is wonderful. May God extend his life and that of his family while he is serving God by serving His people!

- If you are a religious professional, make sure that you give biblical counseling for the glory of God and not for your own gain. I Peter 5:2 says: *"Be shepherds of God's flock that is under your care, serving as overseers-not because you must, but because you are willing, as God wants you to be; not greedy for money, but eager to serve."* Do not separate a husband and wife in order to further your own interest. Remember that God is always watching.

-If you are a Judge, render justice. Do not accept bribes. Proverbs 15:27 says: *"A greedy man brings trouble to his family, but he who hates bribe will live."*

Are You A Born-Again Christian Or A So-Called One?

In II Chronicles 19:6, 7, we read: *"Consider carefully what you do, because you are not judging for man but for the Lord, who is with you whenever you give a verdict. Now let the fear of the Lord be upon you. Judge carefully, for with the Lord our God there is no injustice or partiality or bribery.*

- If you are an attorney, work for your client truthfully, not against him/her by collecting a bigger profit from the insurance company while your client receives nothing. If you act this way, you will not be able to stand the consequences God metes out to you. In Psalm 103:6 the Bible says: *"the Lord works righteousness and justice for all the oppressed."*

- If you are an accountant, calculate the numbers correctly in favor of your client, and not for your own advantage. In I Corinthians 4:2, the Bible says: *"Now it is required that those who have been given a trust must prove faithful."*

- If you are a realtor, a salesperson, an insurance agent, or a professional of some other sort, do the same. Don't let money be your motivation. Tell the truth to your clients. Tell them exactly what you are selling them. Tell them what benefits they will have. Don't pretend to sell them one thing and actually give them something else. If you do so, when they are in trouble, you will be also. My friend, Ernst Safaite, is an Insurance Agent and Mortgage Broker. I have seen him refuse businesses that do not act in the best interest of his clients. He serves in the way he does to please the Lord. He is not motivated by money, but by service. Beloved, if you are a Christian, you need to do the same. In *Habakkuk* 2:9, the Bible says, *"Woe to him who builds his realm by unjust gain to set his nest on high, to escape the clutches of ruin!"*

- If you are a Christian, when you buy something from a department store or some other kind of store, you should keep it unless there is a defect in it. Don't buy a dress to go to a wedding ceremony Saturday night, and then take it back Monday morning as if you did not wear it. That is unethical. The same goes for every thing else.

In Florida, many people go **to Home Depot** and similar stores and buy a generator before the Hurricane season and return it after. That is wrong! When you buy it, you keep it. If you want to return it, you need to rent it for six months for the Hurricane Season, and then you can return it. If not, you need to keep it, because it is yours.

Remember that we should not copy what the world does. We are the models. We are light. We need to shine. Often times you think that you are saving money by doing these things, but in reality you are losing, since you attract the curse of God upon you.

What you're doing is saving pennies against dollars. The Bible says in Proverbs 19:1: *"Better a poor man whose walk is blameless than a fool whose lips are perverse."*

In general, my fellow believers, do not be greedy. The Bible says: *"The love of money is the root of all kinds of evil. Some people, eager for money, have wandered from the faith and pierced themselves with many griefs."(I Timothy 6:10)* Do not use money to tempt people. Do not be corrupt. Live by the word of God. Do not live like the world.

Are You A Born-Again Christian Or A So-Called One?

Money and material possessions might be everything for the world, but not for Christians. We are travelers here below. Our real home is in heaven. Don't live by what some body has called the pig's "motto". My father in law, Jean Saint-Fort, used to work for the state of Haiti. He was once the National Director of Education, and the Minister of Education at that time was Mr. Joseph C. Bernard. The two of them put a plan together to fight corruption. But it was not easy. They were taking a lot of criticism from some employees and from some people who were receiving checks but not doing any work. In reality, it became a struggle of the worst kind. They did all they could to satisfy these folks, including increasing their salary, but still they were unsatisfied.

One day my father in law met with his superior and they discussed what to do next. Then he said to Mr. Bernard, "Uncle Joe (he was an older gentleman), after all we have done to help these people, they are still trying to steal, to cut corners, to grab more and more; and it seems like they will never be satisfied…!"

Then, Mr. Joe Bernard answered and said: "Jean, some people live by the pig's motto: live happy and die fat."

My friend, I know that you get the point. Christians cannot live like that. We live one day at a time. Jesus said: "If we have food and clothing that is enough for us…" Hopefully, English spoken, English understood. May God bless you!

4. What should be the Christian Attitude *Towards* Others?

In Philippians 2:5-8, the Bible says: *"Your attitude should be the same as that of Christ Jesus: Who, being in very nature God, did not consider equality with God something to be grasped, but made himself nothing, taking the very nature of a servant, being made in human likeness. And being found in appearance as a man, he humbled Himself and became obedient to death even death on a cross!"* This passage teaches three attitudes that the Christian should adopt:

A). A Sacrificial Love.

Jesus' love was so deep and so strong that he was willing to die for others. So, our love should be like Jesus' love. You don't have to go to the cross to show that love; but you can demonstrate it by how much you care for others, by how much that you are willing to let go for Christ's sake.

As a Christian, you are going to be attacked by others in many ways. But, how you respond will make the difference. How do you respond to your neighbor's attacks in regards to your children or your pets? You might be a victim of some curse words or bad attitudes from your co-workers or even from your family members or friends. But you need to remember that the Bible says: *"Do not take revenge, my friends, but leave room for God's wrath, for it is written: it is mine to avenge I will repay, says the Lord."* Romans 12:19.

It is natural to feel like we must retaliate; but it takes supernatural grace to leave it in the hands of your righteous God.

Are You A Born-Again Christian Or A So-Called One?

As Christians, we must have the same attitude toward everybody, every race, every nation and every people. Don't pre-judge any person because of place of origin, race, or nationality. Remember that God has His people in every race, people, or nation. Do not discriminate against anybody. Don't show prejudice towards anybody. Jesus Christ did not manifest prejudice and did not practice any form of discrimination or segregation. We need to love, support, appreciate and care for the physically challenged, the elderly, the poor, and orphans, prisoners and foreigners. The Bible says: "for God so loved the world, that He gave His one and only Son…" The world, my beloved, includes every nation, race, and people. As Christians, we must also remember that we cannot take our brother/sister to court. The church board is our court for judgment. And if we take a non-Christian to court or a non-Christian takes us to court, we must win. It is not acceptable for a Christian to lose in court, unless the judge is corrupt in some way. Otherwise, the Christian must win. We have our conscience as our judge. If we do something wrong, the Holy Spirit will let us know that and it is our responsibility to fix it.

If we are at fault, we should know and fix the problem ourselves with the other party. See more details in I Corinthians 6:1-7.

B). **A Humble Spirit of Servanthood.**

If we accept the invitation to be born-again, we must become a servant also. And not only a servant, but a humble one as well. Jesus Christ was a humble servant and so should we.

184

We must be willing to serve others the same way that our Lord would. We must accept sufferings in our service. Our service must include every human being, every social class and every position.

Jesus Christ served all. He helped the lame, the blind, and the paralyzed. He healed the leper. He raised the dead. He fed the hungry. He assisted orphans and widows. He served both the citizens of his country and foreigners. He was a humble missionary. He went everywhere seeking to help others. He showed love, compassion and pity to everyone who needed it. And we are obligated to do the same. We are blessed to have a few of those servants in our church. One of them is Sister Claudette Colinet. The church was born in her house. She is a Registered Nurse (R. N.). She serves everybody, and she serves with zeal. How do you serve? Do you serve everybody? Do you give the glory to God in your service?

As servants of the Lord, we need to be very careful not to fall into the ambush of the evil one. When you serve others as you should, people will appreciate you and the devil won't like that, and he will try to make you feel important so he can trap you. When people appreciate what I have done in serving them and they come to congratulate me, I usually answer in this way: "Glory to God, thank you."

What I try to do is to block the road of temptation so I don't feel that I am important for any reason. When you take the credit for the grace of God working in you, you open the door for Satan, and God who is a jealous God removes His shadow from you and you become vulnerable, and liable to fall into the devil's snare. You become full of pride and arrogant. And guess what? You are about to fall...!

In Proverbs 16:18, the Bible says: *"Pride goes before destruction, a haughty spirit before a fall."*

If you are a married person, remember your vows to your spouse and be very careful when you deal with persons of the opposite sex. Avoid being alone with the opposite sex. If you are single, ask yourself why? Is it because you are called to the single life, or are you not ready for marriage, or are you abusing your position, especially if you are a man?

To become wiser, remember two things. a) We all will give an account of our doings. b) The eyes of the Lord are everywhere at all times.

Last, but not least, when you serve, watch out for the intervention of Satan in the matter of money. If the Lord uses you to pray and bring healing to somebody, don't start charging a fee for your service. If you do, before long you will become useless in the work of the Lord and useful for Satan's.

C). A Commitment to Total Obedience.

The obedience of Jesus Christ to His Father was complete. So should the Christian attitude be to God in everything. We ought to deal with other people as God would Himself. Many people misunderstand what complete obedience is.

We have many cases in the Bible where people thought that they obeyed the Lord, but only to find out later on that they were in total disobedience with the Lord.

In I Samuel 15, we find the case of King Saul. God gave him the order by the prophet Samuel to destroy the Amalekites and everything that belonged to them. But he kept alive the fat animals and even the king, and when Samuel came, he said to him: *"The Lord bless you! I have carried out the Lord's instructions."* I Samuel 15:13

Samuel said: "What then is this bleating of sheep in my ears? What is this lowing of cattle that I hear?" Then, listen to Saul's explanation: "the soldiers **spared the best** of the sheep and cattle to sacrifice to the Lord your God, but we **totally** destroy the rest."

Do you notice how King Saul used the word **"totally"?** God said to destroy everything and everyone **totally.** King Saul destroyed only some of the animals and Amalekites, .but he convinced himself that he had obeyed the Lord completely. Samuel's answer to King Saul was shocking! "Does the Lord delight in burnt offerings and sacrifices as much as in obeying the voice of the Lord? To obey is better than to sacrifice, and to heed is better than the fat of rams. For rebellion is like the sin of divination, and arrogance like the evil of idolatry. Because you have rejected the word of the Lord, ('Guess what') the Lord has rejected you as King." I Samuel 15: 22, 23.

Beloved when we have an obedient attitude toward God, we will have the right attitude toward others as well. The Bible says: "Whatever you do, work at it with all your heart, as working for the Lord, not for men…" Colossians 3:23.

Because Jesus Christ submitted himself totally to the Father, He served others the right way. Though he was serving people, he was pleasing the Father at the same time. In order for us to please God, we have to do as Christ did. And other people will automatically glorify God because of the way we deal with them, when they find out that we are Christians.

187

5. What should be the Christian Attitude Toward his/her Civic Duties?

Many countries around the world are in terrible shape because many Christians believe that it is wrong for the Christian to be involved in politics. This is so wrong. Countries that have Christians as leaders are much better off than countries with non-Christian leaders. The acknowledgement of God and the respect for God bring many benefits to a government.

So if we Christians stay out of politics completely, we leave the door open for Satan to take control of our country.

- Christians need to get involved profoundly in the politics of their country for all the right reasons. You can influence legislation and decision-making and be salt and light wherever you are involved in the government.

- We need to register and vote in every election so that we can elect people with high moral standards. It is not all right when some people say, "I am not going to vote because I don't like either candidate." It is not easy to find somebody with the same point of view as yours. However, you will find good reasons to prefer one candidate over the others.

It is also our responsibility to pray for our government whether it is good or bad. People misunderstand if they pray only for a government they like and don't pray for the one they dislike. The Bible commands us to pray for the government, because whoever the governor is, he is your governor. Your prayer can bring insight for the administration of that particular government.

In I Timothy 2:1-4, the Bible says: *"I urge, then, first of all, that requests, prayers, intercession and thanksgivings be made for everyone-for Kings and all those in authority, that we may live peaceful and quiet lives in all godliness and holiness. This is good, and pleases God our Savior, who wants all men to be saved and to come to knowledge of the truth."*

- We Christians need to submit to our leaders. The Bible says: *"Everyone must submit himself to the governing authorities, for there is no authority except that which God has established. The authorities that exist have been established by God. Consequently, he who rebels against the authority is rebelling against what God has instituted, and those who do so will bring judgment on themselves. For rulers, hold no terror for those who do right, but for those who do wrong. Do you want to be free from fear of the one in authority? Then do what is right and he will commend you; for he is God's servant to do you good. But if you do wrong, be afraid, for he does not bear the sword for nothing. He is God's servant, an agent of wrath to bring punishment on the wrongdoer".*
Romans 13:1-4.

Beloved, we must not forget to apply the word of God in every sphere of our lives. We must show respect and submission to all authorities. They are God's servants and we need to respect them, submit to them and obey their command, unless it is in conflict with the authority of God Himself. And we must do that, whether or not we like the government. Whether the government is legitimate or illegitimate, submit yourself for the Lord's sake to every authority instituted among men. whether to the King, as the supreme authority, or to governors, who are sent by him to punish those who do wrong and to commend those who do right. Remember that all government is established by God. For it is God's will that by doing well you should silence the ignorant talk of foolish men. It may not be God's ideal will, but it is His permissive will for such and such a government to be the ruler of such and such a people. In Daniel 4:17, the Bible declares: *"...The most high is sovereign over the kingdoms of men and gives them to anyone he wishes and sets over them the lowliest of men."*

In Psalm 103:19, the Bible says: *"The Lord has established his throne in heaven, and his kingdom rules over all."*

My friend, let us obey the word of God the best we know how and we will not get ourselves in trouble with the authorities and with God. God honors the laws of countries and when we break the law, we must pay the consequences as well.

Sometimes, we may break the law because of ignorance, but even in that case, we still have to face the consequences. One judge said: "The ignorance of the law does not stop you from paying the penalties of violating the law."

Sometimes, sincerity and honesty might help us when we find a good police officer or a good judge, but only when we tell the truth and we are sorry and apologize for what we have done wrong.

Now more than ever we need to pray for our leaders. After September 11, 2001, the world became a different place and many governments are overreacting in their quest for safety. Unfortunately, some of them take the wrong direction, though not intentionally. They are looking for safety in all the wrong places. I want to give you, heads of states of the world, some advice on the matter of safety. True safety will not come from waging war, nor will it come from concrete walls or fences, neither will it come from surveillance cameras or other human effort. True safety will come from the Lord God Almighty and from Him alone. Solomon was the wisest king who ever lived on the face of the earth (apart from Jesus Christ). Here is what he said: *"Unless the Lord builds the house, its builders labor in vain. Unless the Lord watches over the city, the watchmen stand guard in vain."(Psalm 127:1)* Also there was another wise king by the name of Jehoshaphat, who once had a problem in assuring the safety of his people, the Israelites (Jews). He did have a great army; but he did not rely on the strength of his army. Jehoshaphat decided to seek the help of the Lord. He published a fast for all the people including himself. Here is what he said:

> *O Lord, God of our fathers, are you not the God who is in heaven? You rule over all the kingdoms of the nations. Power and might are in your hand, and no one can withstand you...here are men from Ammon, Moab and Mount Seir, whose territory you would not allow Israel to invade when they came from Egypt; so they turned away from them and did not destroy them. See how they are repaying us by coming to drive us out of the possession you gave us as an inheritance. O our God, will you not judge them? For we have no power to face this vast army that is attacking us. We do not know what to do, but our eyes are upon you." (II Chronicles 20:6, 10 -12).*

Now, check out the answer of the Lord in verse 15, *"Listen, King Jehoshaphat and all who live in Judah and Jerusalem! This is what the Lord says to you: Do not be afraid or discouraged because of this vast army. For the battle is not yours, but God's."* *Because* the king put his trust in the Lord, he was victorious. You can look at his victory in verses 22-24 of the same chapter. You too can be protected if you know where to find real safety. So, the key for safety for the USA and for any other country of the world is to bring back or restore God and the Bible in all of our institutions, public and private. In II Chronicles 7:14 the Bible says: *"If my people, who are called by my name, will humble themselves and pray and seek my face and turn from their wicked ways, then will I hear from heaven and will forgive their sin and will heal their land."* When we do that, we will have complete safety and we can claim these words found in Isaiah 41:10, which says: *"So do not fear, for I am with you; do not be dismayed, for I am your God. I will strengthen you and help you; I will uphold you with my righteous right hand."*

In so saying, I don't want you to think that I am against all wars! I am not. Since sin entered the world, we must have wars when they are necessary to restrain evil. And I salute our troops in Iraq and Afghanistan and anywhere else they might be in the future, for their sacrifices to keep our freedom. Every American should support them. They and their families are continually in our prayers.

I want to give this advice to all Christian nations, especially the USA. Be wise as to how you handle the matter of immigration! Remember that the USA has been and is being built by immigrants and it is the city of refuge for the world. Washington DC is not only the US Capital, but also the Embassy of the world.

Remember that Jesus Christ was an immigrant in Egypt. As a Christian nation, we have the obligation to protect the world by

192

protecting families. The law on immigration should protect the unity of the family. Please always consider the unity of the family in legislating the laws of immigration in our Christian nation. The Bible says: *"Do not deprive each other except by mutual consent and for a time, so that you may devote yourselves to prayer. Then come together again so that Satan will not tempt you because of your lack of self-control."* (I Corinthians 7:5) You might say why is that important? The Bible says in Proverbs 14:34, *"Righteousness exalts a nation, but sin is a disgrace to any people."*

We are praying that the wisdom of God may be upon you while you are trying to do the right thing for all people! May the blessing of the Lord be upon you and yours!

May the Lord our God give us wisdom and understanding to do the right thing in every occasion in order to bring glory to His Holy name!

I want to encourage you in everything that you are doing to do it for the Lord. First, I want you to know that God takes notice. Second, there are people observing and appreciating what you are doing, and they are also praying for you. So, take heart, be courageous and continue to do what you are doing for God' sake. Your reward is and will be great. May the blessings of the Lord be upon you forever!

Are You A Born-Again Christian Or A So-Called One?

CHAPTER TEN

MONEY

1. What is Money?

Someone has said: *"Money is a good servant, but a bad master."* Paul, the apostle said: *"the love of money, not money itself, is the root of all kinds of evil." I Timothy 6:10*

Money is a medium of exchange utilized by people around the world. Money allows people to carry their wealth with them anywhere they go. Nobody can pick up their house or their land and transport them to another location; but they can sell them for money and take the money wherever they go.

Money makes life easy when you use it wisely. In other words, money is a wonderful thing. Everybody dreams of having money, and lots of it. Some people sacrifice their lives for money. Others sacrifice their family for money. The worst are those who damn their souls for the sake of money.

You who are reading this book now, what do you think about money? How much do you like money? Do you prefer money over people? Do you exploit people for money?

I encourage you to make some resolutions now while you do not have much money so you can make better use of it when you do have more money in your possession; if not, you might lose your life and leave your money behind you.

The Bible says: *"For we brought nothing to the world, and we can take nothing out of it." I Timothy 6:7*

A wise person said this about money: "Money can buy medications, but not good health. Money can buy a good bed, but cannot provide sleep. Money can buy food, but not appetite. Money can buy a pair of glasses, but can not give vision."

Don't you think that's true? You and I need to think twice about money and people...when you are in ICU (Intensive Care Unit) in the general hospital of your area, it does not matter how much money you possess, does it!

Money is a god, but a powerless one when you are in real trouble. Money is unable to give you any lasting peace.

I hope that by reading this, you will begin to think more rationally about money!

2. Is Money your Servant or your Master?

Jesus Christ, in His earthy ministry, met a young rich man who asked Him: *"Good teacher, what must I do to inherit eternal life?"*

And Jesus answered: "...You know the commandments: Do not commit adultery, do not murder, do not steal, do not give false testimony, honor your father and mother."

The man replied: "All these I kept since I was a boy." Then Jesus said to him: "you still lack one thing. Sell everything you have and give to the poor, and you will have treasure in heaven. Then come and follow me." Luc 18:18-22.

Do you remember the reaction of that man? The Bible says: *"He became very sad, because he was a man of great wealth."* Luc 18:23.

What Jesus did to that man back then, we could say to him today, "I gotcha!"

That is exactly what Jesus did to the rich man. He tried to make himself appear to be a perfect man, a man who believed in God when in reality he believed in his money. Money was his god. Jesus knew it all along, and that is why He hit him right on the money. Who is your God, by the way? Is the Triune God your God, or is money your god? I was told a story about a man by the name of Paul Getty, who was very rich, who, in fact worshiped money. At least he did so at a certain time in his life. This man was so concerned about his money that he installed a pay phone in his house so that when he invited guests, they would not have to use his telephone, and he could also make a profit from his guests. Believe it or not, this is a true story.

Jesus said: *"No one can serve two masters. Either he will hate the one and love the other or he will be devoted to the one and despise the other. You can not serve both God and money."* Matthew 6:24.

Are you aware of the reality that Jesus knows exactly who you are? He knows if you are a born again Christian who serves only God or if you are fooling yourself. You can fool your pastor, your Sunday school teacher, your fellow church member, but you cannot fool God.

Remember what the Bible says: *"Do not be deceived: God can not be mocked. A man reaps what he sows."* There is a Haitian Proverbs that says: "A leaky house can fool the sun, but not the rain."

If money is your god, you can hide that fact for years. But remember that you can only do it for so long during a sunny season; and then the rainy season will come shortly; so be aware!

If you are not careful, what happened to the rich young man will happen to you also. He was rich on earth, but poor in hell. The same can happen to you.

3. Who is the Real Owner of your Money?

We usually fool ourselves by saying or thinking that the money we have belongs to us. We brag about it and we use it to show our superiority over others. And the only reason we do that is **ignorance.** We don't know God really, nor His word.

In Psalms 24:1, we read: *"The earth is the Lord's, and everything in it, the world, and all who live in it."*

In Deuteronomy 8:18, the Bible declares: *"Remember the Lord your God, for it is he who gives you the ability to produce wealth…"*

In I Corinthians 10:26, we read: *"the earth is the Lord's, and everything in it."*

Also, in I Corinthians 4:7, we find this question: *"…what do you have that you did not receive? And if you did receive it, why do you boast as though you did not?"*

Beloved, do you understand what you've just read? Will you come to your senses? Do you realize that you really own nothing? Do you know that God holds in His hand right now the breath of your life? It is like a switch with three positions.

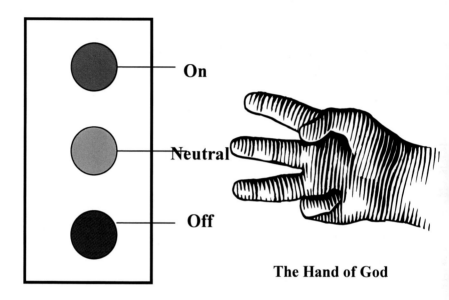

On

Neutral

Off

The Hand of God

Your life switch

The reason why you are boasting so much is the fact that God keeps the switch on the "On" position. If God put it in "Neutral", you would be in trouble, maybe laying down on a bed at home or in the hospital, where you can do nothing for yourself. And if God decides to turn it on the "Off" position, you are gone, you cease to live, you are a dead person. Have you thought about it this way?

199

If you do, you will be wiser. You will think before you act. And you will have a better life on earth and possibly in heaven as well.

My friend, God is not only the real owner of your money, He also owns you. He is your creator. You are merely a creature.

You are but a manager, a steward of the money in your possession. You will have to give an account about how you utilize it. Do you remember the parable of the talents recorded in Matthew 25:14-30? Jesus gave some talents to three men. To one He gave five talents, to another He gave two talents, and to another one he gave one talent. They were to make them worth more. Two of the three men did a good job, they doubled the worth of them, but the third man did not.

When the time came to give an account of their administration, two were found faithful and one unfaithful. Jesus gave this parable for us, you and me, and everybody else.

For every dollar that comes into our possession, we will have to give an account to Jesus when He comes again. Will you be ready to do that? The money you have now is your talent. That includes your house or houses, your land, your cars, your bank accounts, your stocks, your savings bonds, your jewelry, your expensive furniture, your lavish vacations, your education, your position in life in religion, in politics and in business. Did you know that?

Do you keep a good record? Do you make good use of the master's money?

If not, you need to start now. How?

(1) Acknowledge to Jesus that you were not acting as a steward, but as an owner.

(2) Confess to Him this sin and ask for His forgiveness.

(3) Ask Him to help you, to show you how he wants you to utilize his money.

(4) And make a vow to do only His will, not your own

4. Do you pay tithes and offerings in your church?

I have heard many arguments about paying tithes to the church by many so-called Christians.

The first one I heard is: "The tithe is the law." The second one is, "The tithe is Biblical, but not Evangelical." The third one is, "The tithe is a voluntary thing," if you want to pay the tithe you can, but if you don't want to, you don't have to. The fourth one is: "Some people think that they are too poor to pay tithe." The fifth is, "The church is rich, so it does not need the money," so they can keep it for themselves. I believe that there are more. However, I am going to respond to these five.

(1) Let me begin by teaching you something you do not know or you choose to ignore. The tithe is not the law. The tithe existed more than four hundred years before the law. In Genesis 14:20, we read: *"And blessed be God most high, who delivered your enemies into your hand. Then Abram gave him a tenth of everything."* Jacob did the same thing. In Genesis 28:22, we find these words: *"And this stone that I have set up as a pillar will be God's house, and all that you give me I will give you a tenth."* The tithe began with Abraham, the friend of God, who had faith in God, and honored Him with a tenth of all God's blessings in his life. It was a way to show respect and gratitude to God.

Remember that, the tithe is not the law. The tithe existed a long, long time before the law was given.

(2) The tithe is both Biblical and Evangelical. The Bible is a whole. The true believer embraces the Old and the New Testaments. The born-again Christian trusts the Bible from Genesis one to Revelation twenty-two.

(3) Abraham was the first to pay the tithe. Abraham is the father of all who believe; Jews and Christians are both descendants of Abraham. In Romans 4:11, we read: *"...so then he (Abraham) is the father of all who believe..."* and in verses 16 and 17, we read: *"therefore, the promise comes by faith, so that it may be by grace and may be guaranteed to all Abraham's offspring, not only to those who are of the law but also to those who are of the faith of Abraham. He is the father of us all. As it is written: I have made you a father of many nations..."*

In the Bible, God called those who said that they believe in God and do not do what He commands liars. He calls those who don't pay their tithes, robbers. In Malachi 3:7-10, we read: *"Ever since the time of your forefathers you have turned away from my decrees and have not kept them. Return to me, and I will return to you, says the Lord Almighty. But you ask how are we to return? Will a man rob God? Yes you rob me. But you ask, how do we rob you? In tithes and offerings. You are under a curse-the whole nation of you –because you are robbing me. Bring the whole tithe into the store house, that there may be food in my house. Test me in this, says the Lord Almighty, and see if I will not throw open the floodgates of heaven and pour out so much blessing that you will not have room enough for it."*

Level 1 **Level 2** **Level 3**

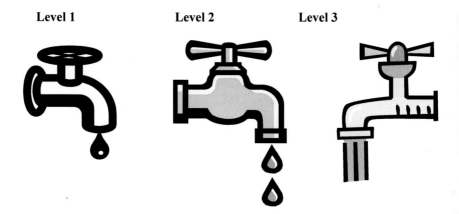

Choose the level of your blessings.

The Pharisees wanted to trap Jesus when they sent disciples to ask Him a question about paying taxes to Caesar. In Matthew 22:17, 20, 21, they asked Jesus: *"Tell us then, what is your opinion? Is it right to pay taxes to Caesar or not?" After Jesus rebuked them for their hypocrisy, he asked them for a coin. "Whose portrait is this? and whose inscription?" he asked them. "Caesar's," they replied. Then Jesus said to them: "Give to Caesar what is Caesar's, and to God what is God's."*

Caesar received taxes, and God receives tithes and offerings.

Jesus also rebuked the teachers of the law, when they put more emphasis on tithing and neglected justice, mercy and faithfulness. He told them that both were important. *"...you should have practiced the latter, without neglecting the former."* Matthew 23:23.

Are You A Born-Again Christian Or A So-Called One?

My friend, the tithe is Biblical and Evangelical. Every Christian **must** pay tithes and offerings and add on top of that some gifts periodically according to how the Lord has blessed him.

Let me make it clear, very clear to you. If you are a Christian and you do not pay tithes, it is because of **one thing**. Do you want to know what this one thing is? I believe that you do. The one thing is **ignorance**. Ignorance is the only thing that can keep a Christian from paying tithes. If after you have received the teachings about paying your tithes and offerings and you are still not doing it, my friend, there is only **one** reason: You are not a **born-again Christian**, you are a **so-called one**. In other words, money is your real god. I am sorry if I hurt your feeling, but it is better for you to get hurt now than later. Do you remember what Paul told the Corinthians **on one** occasion after an exhortation? II Corinthians 7:8-10 says, *"Even if I caused you sorrow by my letter, I do not regret it. Though I did regret it - I see that my letter hurt you, but only for a little while - yet now I am happy, not because you were made sorry, but because your sorrow led you to repentance. For you became sorrowful as God intended and so were not harmed in any way by us. Godly sorrow brings repentance that leads to salvation and leaves no regret, but worldly sorrow brings death."*

If you cannot give 10% of God's money back to God's Kingdom, it is because you are a thief. There is no room in heaven for robbers. I hope and pray that you do the right thing.

As Christians, we are supposed to give more than the Jews. The Jews gave 23⅓% as their tithes, and we Christians are unwilling to give 10%. This is a **crime** against the church of Jesus Christ.

Someone must be willing to tell you that, and I am "proudly humbled" to be one of the persons to tell you. I know that God will bless me for that. If you want to verify that you have in your hand the faucet of blessings, go and read for yourself the story of the widow's oil in II Kings 4:1-7.

This was a widow who had two sons. After the death of her husband, the creditor of her husband wanted to make her two sons slaves in order to work to pay off the debt they owed. She cried out to Elisha, the prophet of God. She was a faithful lady and wife of a faithful man of God. Then, Elisha asked her, what do you have in your house? She said, your servant has nothing, except for a little oil. Do you notice the truthfulness and faithfulness of that lady? Are you as truthful and faithful as her? Think about it! Because she was honest, Elisha told her, go to you neighbors and borrow as many empty jars as possible. Then, go inside your house and close your doors behind you and your sons. And pour oil into all the jars one after the other. She did as she was told. As soon as one was full she asked for another one. The oil kept on pouring. Finally, when she asked for another jar, the children answered, there are no more; and the oil stopped. Beloved, do you get it? She had measured her blessings by how many jars that she had collected. It is the same thing for you and me. We measure our blessings by how faithful we are in obeying the commands of Jesus Christ. The law of giving and receiving is the same with natural law; your sowing will determine your harvest here on earth and in heaven. If somebody asked you: "How much do you invest in the Kingdom of God?" how would you answer this question?

(4) If you think that the tithe is voluntary, my friend, you are mistaken about what is mandatory and what is voluntary. **Salvation is voluntary.** No one can force you to save yourself. But the **tithe is mandatory** for every born-again Christian. It may be voluntary for the so-called one, but not for the authentic Christian.

Jesus gave a command when He said: *"Give to Caesar, what is Caesar's, and to God, what is God's."* He did not make a suggestion.

Saying that you pay tithes only if you want to… this is heresy. It is like saying you can stop for a red light only if you want to. They are both deadly. One is physical and the other is spiritual. You don't want to pay tithes because you are not born of the spirit of God; yet the consequences of that is eternal damnation.

My friend, if you thought that paying tithes was optional; know that, it is not so for the true believer. We born-again Christians listen to and practice the word of God, and we obey faithfully His commands.

(5) Some people think that they are too poor to pay tithes. The worst of that is the fact that some preachers agree with this idea. I tell you the truth, I am so sorry for both of you (preacher and believer) that I am crying out of pity for you both while I am writing this.

Let me ask you a question: If you make $100.00 a week, wouldn't you be able to live on $80.00? If you were to give $10.00 for your tithes and $10.00 for your offerings, wouldn't you be able to survive with the $80.00, which is left?

Well, if you cannot survive with $80.00, then you would not be able to survive with $100.00 either.

Whatever amount of money you make, you owe a minimum of 10% of it to the person who **holds your oxygen tube in His hands**; plus a voluntary offering. The tithe is mandatory to guarantee a certain amount of money coming to the church of God regularly, and offerings are also mandatory with the only difference being that your generosity is measured by the amount you give.

Do you know why you think that you are too poor to give to the work of God?

One reason: Your heart is not yet touched by the Spirit of God…That is it. No other reason, and I am basing this on experience, not just speaking theoretically. The **people who give** more money to the church are the **poor people**. I have one lady in the church that I serve whose name is Liliane Hypolite. She is a widow according to the *biblical* standard. She does not work. She occasionally watches over a child for a friend or a family member. Her job is offering daily prayers for the saints. And do you know that she gives regularly to the church.

I know what you might think…maybe she has some investments and she receives some returns…no, not at all. She lives with her daughter and son in law. She does not have a bank account. The last time we had building fund raising, she brought an old envelope to me and said: "Servant of God, here is my bank." I told her, "God will give you a brand new one. You close your envelope's bank for God's work, but He will reopen it very soon." And God did. She is still giving.

I say that to let you know for certain that you are not too poor to give tithes and offerings to God's Kingdom. The only thing that would prevent you from doing that after you have received teachings on this subject is that you have not been converted.

(6) Some people claim that the church is rich, so they do not have to give to the church anymore. Let me ask you something: "Where in the Bible did Jesus say to stop giving to the church when that institution becomes too rich?"

What kind of riches are you talking about? How many churches do you know without some poor people in them?

If the church is so rich, then how come the church still has poor people in it?

How come the church is so rich and we have thousands of pastors who are serving a congregation and are still working outside the church to provide for their family? I am one of them.

Do you know that when they pass the collection basket in the majority if not all churches, **only about 15 to 20% of the people give something?**

Do you know that some people pretend with their hands to put in something, but they do not put anything in?

Plus, if the church you go to is rich, it could be richer if you would give as you are commanded to do.

My friend, every time you think about all kinds of excuses not to give, remember that God said: *"Bring all the tithes and the offerings to the storehouse*
so that there is food in my house." Malachi 3:10.

Beloved, if you are born again Christians, obey the word of God. Do as you are told by the Scriptures. If you are not one, I encourage you to give your heart truly to Jesus Christ and be born again. If you do that, you won't have any more excuses not to give money to the church to further the work of the kingdom of Jehovah. For those of you who are bragging that you don't give tithes and offerings and you are still blessed, let me tell you why. It is because you are not in, and God pays no attention to you. But if you were in, you would have received the rebuke of God.

I have a brother in our church by the name of Francois Florvilus. His wife Vonnie is a board member. There are very faithful people. They pay their tithes and offerings and give gifts on top of that regularly. One day, Bro. Francois was driving and he got a flat tire. When he got back home, he did not have any money in the house but the tithe. So, he decided to take some money from the tithe to buy a new tire for his car; however, he did not intend to replace it. The Bible does allow us to borrow from our tithes, but we must pay it back with an interest of a fifth of the value (Leviticus 27:31).

But this was not the case for my dear brother. Guess what! He took the money, bought a new tire and drove for about 5 miles, and the new tire blew up.

Now, you might say, this is a coincidence! I will respond in this way: if God cares about you, He wants to bless you. When He realizes that you are falling from his blessings, He brings you back to your Christian obligations and to your obedience to Him. So, my friends, when you do what is wrong with your tithes and nothing happens, it is not a sign that everything is fine with God, but a sign that everything is wrong with you.

There are many more excuses used by so-called Christians, but I chose to talk about five of them, and I hope that, that will help you to see clearly so you can stop fooling yourself.

In a discussion about tithes and offerings we had in our church sometime in the past, one lady asked me if it was a sin to send her tithe to her homeland…I said, it depends on how you define sin. If sin is disobedience to what God said, then it is sin. The storehouse is where you go to worship God, not your homeland. Plus if something happened to you, you cannot call your homeland for assistance, but you can come to the church.

My friend, you need to pay **the tithe to your local church**. It is a command from God. And you need to do that **with all your heart, and regularly**. Let us be good stewards of the money God gives us and we will reap the benefits one day in heaven.

5. How should the Christian give?

The true believer must always think about giving…Christianity is tied to giving. God is the greatest giver. He showed that to us when He gave His only begotten Son to die in our place. Jesus was His one and only Son. We read in John 3:16: "For God so loved that He gave His one and only Son."

When you become a born again Christian, you have automatically experienced a change of heart. You see things differently. You begin to see things the way God would see them. Because of the work of the Holy Ghost in you, you begin to have a desire to give, to help and to assist others in difficulty or in trouble and you want to act like the Macedonians. In II Corinthians 8:1, 2, we read, *"And now, brothers, we want you to know about the grace that God has given the Macedonian churches out of the most severe trial, their overflowing joy and their extreme poverty welled up in rich generosity."* They were eager to give to help the saints.

You and I, are we eager to give to further the work of the Kingdom?

They gave generously to the collection in favor of other believers in need. As to us today, how do we give, liberally or sparingly?

Firstly, a Christian must give generously.

In II Corinthians 9:6, we read: *"Whoever sows sparingly will also reap sparingly, and whoever sows generously will also reap generously."*

How you sow will determine your crop...everything you do in life is a kind of sowing, and there will be a crop at the end. If you are a born again Christian, generosity must be your friend. If not, check your heart out!

Secondly, a Christian must give regularly.

In I Corinthians 16:2, the Bible says: *"On the first day of every week, each one of you should set aside a sum of money in keeping with his income, saving it up, so that when I come no collections will have to be made."*

You need to give as you have received. If you are paid every week, you need to give every week also; or if you receive gifts or assistance

211

every month, you need to give to church monthly. Whatever the Christian receives, he/she can give back to the Lord. What you receive is from the Lord Himself. He utilizes human channels to bring it to you and he is watching your response to Him when it comes for you to give back to Him through His church.

Thirdly, the Christian must give sacrificially.

Do you remember the case of Elijah and the widow of Zarephath? When God sent Elijah to Zarephath to the home of a widow, He knew that widow would give to God from whatever she possessed. So God sent His servant to her. And she only had enough flour and oil to make two small cakes, one for her and one for her son, and after that they expected to die of hunger. However, when the man of God showed up, he asked her to make the first one for him and then make two others after that. That was sacrificial giving, wasn't it?

By making the first one for Elijah, there might seem to be enough to make just one more, implying that she would have to share one with her son. But, guess what? She did it anyway. And because of her sacrificial giving, God provided for her and her son until the coming of rain and the harvest of the land.

My friend, do you think that it is important to give sacrificially? I think that it is indispensable for the Christian. The Macedonians did exactly that. In II Corinthians 8:3-5, we read: *"For I testify that they gave as much as they were able, and even beyond their ability. Entirely on their own, they urgently pleaded with us for the privilege of sharing in this service to the saints. And they did not do as we expected, but they gave themselves first to the Lord and then to us in keeping with God's will."*

Do you remember the widow in Jesus' time who gave sacrificially?

Fourthly, the Christian must give joyfully.

Some people give only to attract a curse upon themselves. They give against their will. Please, don't do that. You should give only if your heart prompts you to give. The Bible says in II Corinthians 9:7: *"Each man should give what he has decided in his heart to give, not reluctantly or under compulsion, for God loves a cheerful giver."*

Beloved, when you give generously, regularly, sacrificially and joyfully, you prove that you are: 1) a born again Christian, 2) faithful and obedient to the commands of the Lord, your master, 3) under the blessings of the Lord or a candidate to receive them, 4) helping further the work of the Kingdom, 5) and one day going to heaven with God.

In other words, dear co-laborer in Christ, take heart, keep doing good works, press on and I will see you in heaven. May God bless you!

Are You A Born-Again Christian Or A So-Called One?

THE TEN COMMANDMENTS

- You shall have no other gods before me
- You shall not make for yourself a carved image; nor shall you bow down or serve them.
- You shall not take the name of the Lord your God in vain.
- Remember the Sabbath day to keep it holy.
- Honor your father and your mother that your days may be long upon the land.
- You shall not murder
- You shall not commit adultery
- You shall not steal
- You shall not bear false witness against your neighbor.
- You shall not covet your neighbor's thing.

NKJV.

The Greatest Commandments according to Jesus.

1. "Love the Lord your God with all your heart and with all your soul and with all your mind and with all your strength.
2. Love your neighbor as yourself.

There is no commandment greater than these." Mark 12:30, 31

NOTES

CHAPTER 1

1. Notre pain quotidien-Our Daily Bread, Vol.8-Publications Chrétiennes Inc.-Christian Publications Inc. (Grand Rapids, MI: Radio Bible Class, 1997) Feb.3rd.

2. The Eerdman Bible Dictionary –(Grand Rapids, MI, William B. Eerdmans Publishing Company- 1987) p.147.

3. Robert Boyd, The World Bible Handbook –(Grand Rapids, MI: World Publishing, 1991) p. 19.

4. The Eerdman Bible Dictionary, p.523.

5. Michael C. Bere, Bible Doctrine for Today (Pensacola, FL, Pensacola Christian College-A Beka Book- 1996) p. 14.

6. Georges Sweeting, Who Said That? (Chicago, Moody Press. 1985) p. 61.

7. Help me Howard (Television Channel 7, in 2004).

8. D. James Kennedy, Why I Believe (Dallas-London-Vancouver-Melbourne, Word Publishing, 1980) p. 26.

Chapter 2

1. The Eerdman Bible Dictionary, p. 243.

2. R.C. Sproul, Essential Truths of the Christian Faith (Wheaton IL., Tyndale House Publishers, Inc., 1992) p. 37.

3. Notre Pain Quotidien-Our Daily Bread, Vol.8.) March 3rd.

4. Sweeting, Who Said That?, p. 129.

5. John Haggee's Preachings, Trinity Broadcasting Network

Chapter 3

1. Haitian Proverb

2. Stanley A. Ellisen, Connaitre La Parole de Dieu- Knowing God's Word (Deerfield, FL, Vida, 1990) p. 24.

3. Nouveau Dictionaire Biblique-New Bible Dictionary (Saint-Leger Sur Vevey, Suisse :Editions Emmaus, 1806) pp. 426, 427.

4. New Scofield Reference Bible, (French Edition) (Genève, Paris : La Société Biblique de Genève); Diffusion: La Maison de la Bible, 1975) p. 406.

Chapter 4

1. Frank Reidorf-Reece, Encyclopedie Biblique-Bible Encyclopedia (La Begude de Mazenc, France 26160 :La Croisade Du Livre Chretien, 1974) p.166.

2. Notre Pain Quotidien-Our Daily Bread, Vol.8, Oct.24.

3. Billy Graham crusade, North Dakota, 1987.

Chapter 5

1. Sweeting, Who Said That? p. 401.

2. Ibid., p. 402.

Chapter 6

1. New Scofield Reference Bible (French Edition) p. 1390.

Chapter 7

1. Sweeting, Who Said That? p. 386.

2. Chœur Français- French chorus (Chants d'Espérance-Songs of Hope, No 10)

3. Sweeting, Who Said That? p. 386.

4. Ibid., p. 385.

Chapter 8

1. Michael Griffiths, Belle, mais Délaissée- Beautiful, but Abandonned (Mulhouse, Cedex 68059, France, Editions: Grâce et Vérité- 1985) p. 5.

2. Vivian Bernstein, America's History, Land of Liberty (Steck-Vaughn Company, 1997) p. 93.

3. Ibid., p. 97

4. Robert Turner, Jr., Study Guide, American History (Harcourt Learning Direct Publications, Inc., 1998) p. 37.

Are You A Born-Again Christian Or A So-Called One?